GUERRILLA AND COUNTERGUERRILLA

WARFARE IN GREECE, 1941 - 1945

by

Hugh H. Gardner

OFFICE OF THE CHIEF OF MILITARY HISTORY
Department of the Army
Washington, D.C., 1962

This manuscript has been prepared in the Office of the Chief of Military History, Department of the Army, for use by the Special Warfare School, Special Warfare Center, Fort Bragg, N.C. <u>Guerrilla and Counterguerrilla Warfare in Greece, 1941 - 1945</u> constitutes the first part of a projected volume to contain histories of a number of guerrilla movements. In order that material contained in this portion may be made available to the Special Warfare School without delay, the author's first draft is being released prior to being fully reviewed and edited. The manuscript cannot, therefore, be considered or accepted as an official publication of the Office of the Chief of Military History.

GUERRILA AND COUNTERGUERRILLA WARFARE

PART I - GREECE

TABLE OF CONTENTS

| Chapter | | Page |
|---|---|---|
| I | INVASION AND RESISTANCE (1940 - 1942) | 1 |
| | Introduction | 1 |
| | The Geography | 2 |
| | The Economy | 4 |
| | Ethnic and Political Background | 5 |
| | Italy and Germany Attack | 6 |
| | Greece in Defeat | 9 |
| | Development of the Resistance Movement | 12 |
| | Appearance of Overt Resistance | 14 |
| | The Guerrilla Organizations | 17 |
| | ELAS | 18 |
| | EDES | 20 |
| | EKKA | 22 |
| | Other Andarte Organizations | 22 |
| | Outside Influences on the Development of the Guerrilla Movement | 25 |
| | Guerrilla Leadership | 26 |
| | Guerrilla Headquarters | 34 |
| | Supply and Headquarters Security | 36 |
| | Evacuation of Wounded and Medical Care | 38 |
| | Communications and Security | 39 |
| | Recruiting | 42 |
| | Weapons | 46 |
| | Training and Discipline | 47 |
| | Civilian Support | 51 |
| II | EARLY OPERATIONS AND LIAISON WITH THE BRITISH (1942) | 57 |
| | The Occupation | 57 |
| | Louros Gorge Ambush | 59 |
| | Liaison with the British Middle East Command | 66 |
| | British Preparations to Effect Liaison | 69 |
| | Entry of the Liaison Officers | 71 |
| | Preparations for the Viaduct Operation | 75 |
| | Destruction of the Gorgopotamos Viaduct | 79 |
| | After Gorgopotamos | 86 |
| III | NEW MISSIONS AND ATTEMPTS AT UNIFICATION (1943) | 91 |
| | The British Military Mission Remains | 91 |
| | Efforts to Achieve Unification | 95 |

| Chapter | | Page |
|---|---|---|
| III | ELAS and the National Bands Agreement | 98 |
| | ELAS General Headquarters | 104 |
| | Further Efforts at Unification | 106 |
| | Destruction of Asopos Viaduct | 110 |
| | Widespread Sabotage | 113 |
| | The National Bands Agreement Signed | 116 |
| | Establishment of the Joint General Headquarters | 118 |
| | Politics and the Neraidha Airstrip | 121 |
| IV | REORGANIZATION AND REPRISALS (1943 - 1944) | 128 |
| | Reorganization of the German Forces | 128 |
| | Reorganization of the Guerrilla Forces | 131 |
| | The Italian Surrender | 132 |
| | Formation of the Allied Military Mission | 134 |
| | The Pinerolo Division Dissolved | 135 |
| | Fighting Between EDES and ELAS | 136 |
| | German Highway Opening Operations | 137 |
| | Counterguerrilla Security Measures | 139 |
| | Collaborators and the Security Battalions | 140 |
| | Collaboration by Guerrilla Bands | 142 |
| | The Plaka Armistice | 145 |
| | German Counterguerrilla Measures | 150 |
| | German Reprisals Against Civilians | 153 |
| | Counterguerrilla Measures in the Peloponnesus | 155 |
| | Punitive Expeditions and Massacres | 158 |
| V | GUERRILLA AND COUNTERGUERRILLA OPERATIONS (1944) | 162 |
| | Planning for Operation NOAH'S ARK | 162 |
| | Provisional Government for Free Greece | 166 |
| | Changes in ELAS | 168 |
| | The Greek Army Mutiny | 171 |
| | Further Territorial Disputes | 172 |
| | Government of National Unity | 173 |
| | EDES Again Expands | 174 |
| | Operation STEINADLER (Stone Eagle) | 175 |
| | Soviet Liaison Mission | 180 |
| | Operation KREUZOTTER (Viper) | 181 |
| | EAM/ELAS Change of Heart | 185 |
| VI | LIBERATION AND POLITICS (1944 - 1945) | 187 |
| | Operation NOAH'S ARK | 187 |
| | The Caserta Agreement | 189 |
| | The German Exodus | 191 |
| | Results of NOAH'S ARK | 193 |
| | Maintenance of Public Order | 194 |
| | Political Maneuvering in Athens | 196 |
| | The Demobilization Controversy | 198 |
| | Disorders in Athens | 202 |
| | Civil War in Athens | 204 |
| | ELAS Operations Outside of Athens | 206 |
| | Peacemaking Efforts | 210 |
| | The British Offensive | 211 |
| | The Varkiza Agreement | 213 |

## MAPS

| No. | | Following Page |
|---|---|---|
| 1. | Greece - Spheres of Occupation | 8 |
| 2. | The Mount Giona and Viaduct Areas | 70 |
| 3. | Operation STEINADLER | 176 |
| 4. | Operation KREUZOTTER | 182 |

## ILLUSTRATIONS

| | |
|---|---|
| GREECE -- A land of rugged mountains | 2 |
| Side Elevation of GORGOPOTAMOS Viaduct (Reproduction of blueprint) | 76 |
| Side Elevation of ASOPOS Viaduct (Reproduction of blueprint) | 110 |

ASOPOS Viaduct

| | |
|---|---|
| 23 June - Dropped span and wreckage of cantilever support | 112 |
| 2 July - Debris cleared for erection of south end emergency supports | 112 |
| 15 July - Repairs in progress. New supports being constructed at north end | 112 |
| 26 July - Over a month after the sabotage operation. Repairs still incomplete | 112 |

PART I - GREECE

CHAPTER I

INVASION AND RESISTANCE
(1940 - 1942)

## Introduction

Just as the Western World is indebted to the Greeks for many classic examples of art and literature, so it is in their debt for classic examples of unconventional warfare. Frequently attacked and continually threatened by powerful neighbors, Greece has often found it expedient to resort to unconventional methods of warfare to defend or liberate its soil.

Although examples of the employment of unconventional warfare can be cited from many periods of Greek history, no period is of greater interest than the years 1941 to 1950. The history of Greece during World War II and the years immediately following, presents not only examples of guerrilla and counterguerrilla operations, but also clearly illustrates the result of failing to disarm and completely inactivate a guerrilla force at the conclusion of a war. During this brief period a complete cycle of a resistance movement can be traced: the organization of covert resistance, its development into overt guerrilla warfare, guerrilla participation in the liberation of the nation, the attempt of the resistance organization to use its guerrilla force to seize the reins of government, the resulting civil war, and the eventual downfall of the resistance movement.

Since much of the Greek resistance movement was initiated or dominated by the Greek Communist Party, the resistance cycle is also of interest in that it shows the standard techniques advocated by the Cominform for taking advantage of a critical situation to establish a Communistic form of government. The story of the fight to thwart Communist domination of Greece is of particular interest to students of United States military history since the accomplishment of the final phase of that fight -- the destruction of the Communist guerrilla forces -- came largely as a result of U.S. economic and military assistance.

## The Geography

Greece occupies that lower extremity of the Balkan Peninsula which juts out into the Mediterranean from the main mass of eastern Europe. The mainland and the many island groups which form an integral part of Greece have an area of approximately 51,000 square miles, of which the islands represent a little less than one-fifth -- about 9,000 square miles.

Mountains dominate the entire country, the most important range being the Pindus. An extension of the Balkans, the Pindus Range runs north and south through the western half of the peninsula as far south as the Bay of Corinth. Other smaller mountain groups, outcroppings of the Pindus Range, project into the eastern part of the peninsula and south into the Peloponnesus. The islands, too, are either mountainous or extremely hilly. The mountains of Greece are almost invariably rugged, rocky formations and, although some portions are heavily wooded, much of the mountain country has been almost completely deforested.

GREECE -- A land of rugged mountains

For the purposes of this study, mainland Greece can be conveniently divided into five principal areas which are historical as well as geographic entities.

The Peloponnesus, the southern extension of the Greek peninsula, is connected to the rest of the mainland by the narrow Isthmus of Corinth, which is cut by the Corinth Canal. Like the balance of the country, the Peloponnesus is generally mountainous, although it has some coastal plains and a few level valleys scattered throughout the mountains.

Central Greece is considered to be that portion extending from the Gulf of Corinth north to the Othrys Mountain Range, which runs eastward from the Pindus Range to form the southern boundary of Thessaly. Athens, the capital and largest city of Greece, is located in the southeastern corner of the central area. The long, narrow island of Euboea lies close and parallel to the eastern coast, generally considered as a part of central Greece. While Euboea and the mainland portion are both mountainous, there are some wide valleys and coastal plains.

The third area, Thessaly, is a wedge-shaped sector, extending north from the Othrys Range to a line drawn generally from the vicinity of Metsovon northeast to the city of Katerini on the Gulf of Thermaikos on the east coast. The western part of Thessaly is extremely mountainous, but the eastern part contains two large basin areas.

The fourth mainland area is composed of the district of Epirus, an almost entirely mountainous region which lies between Thessaly and the Ionian Sea, and extends from the Gulf of Arta north to Albania.

The fifth area is comprised of Macedonia and Greek Thrace. Western

Macedonia is almost entirely mountainous, but in eastern Macedonia there is a large, level basin area to the north and west of Salonika, the second largest Greek city. Greek Thrace, which extends from Macedonia to the Turkish border is also mountainous. This northernmost part of Greece is bounded on the west by Epirus and Albania, on the north by Jugoslavia and Bulgaria, and on the east by Turkey.

The Economy

While fishing is an important local industry in the islands and along the mainland coast, the lack of suitable harbors had prevented ocean commerce from becoming a major economic factor except at Athens-Piraeus and Salonika.[1] There is little manufacturing other than local light industry and, although only one-fifth of the country is arable, the economy of Greece is based primarily on agriculture, with approximately 75 percent of its eight million people being rural. Sheep and goat raising are the most profitable occupations of those who reside in the mountain areas. Exports of wool, goat hair, and leather are important commercially, but the meager crops, scratched out of mountain garden patches, are entirely for local consumption.

In 1941, Greece had only 1,700 miles of railroads, many of which were narrow gauge. Its one main line was an extension of the railroad running south from Belgrade, across the Greek border to Salonika, and then meandering through the mountains to Athens-Piraeus. There were few paved motor roads or through highways. The failure to develop a network of railroads or paved highways had discouraged the economic growth of the rural areas and, with the farmers lacking easily accessible major markets and the mountain dwellers barely capable of eking out an existence, the living standard of the majority of the people was understandably low.

## Ethnic and Political Background

The present Greek nation is of comparatively recent origin, its greatest expansion having taken place in the late 19th and early 20th Centuries. In 1832, at the conclusion of the Greek War of Independence and the establishment of the Kingdom, Greece consisted only of that part of the peninsula lying south of Thessaly and a number of Aegean islands immediately adjacent to the Greek shores. The Ionian Islands were ceded by Great Britain in 1864, and Thessaly was added in 1881. In 1913, Epirus and Macedonia as well as the islands of Crete, Lesbos, Samothrace, Chios, Lemnos and a number of smaller islands were added as a result of the Balkan Wars. Western Thrace became a part of Greece in 1922 and the Dodecannese Islands were annexed from Italy following World War II.

By 1941, a series of forced as well as voluntary repatriations had largely eliminated ethnic differences in the more recently added territories, although several areas still harbored sizable racial minorities which were highly nationalistic and resented the authority of Athens.

To the minor problem of ethnological differences was added the major problem of strong political differences which had driven wedges even between those who considered themselves purely Grecian in blood and heritage. It has been said in jest that the number of political parties in Greece is roughly equal to the number of inhabitants. Although an obvious exaggeration, the jest contains an element of truth, as witnessed by the fact that as many as 60 political parties have been represented in one Greek national election. This preoccupation with politics had an important bearing on the development of the resistance movement. If the Greek resistance was less effective than it might have been, the blame may be laid at the door of politics -- not lack of patriotism or ethnic differences.

## Italy and Germany Attack

On the eve of World War II, chaotic conditions in Greece, caused by violent and seemingly irreconcilable political differences, so bitter as to threaten armed revolt, had resulted in King George II acquiescing in the establishment of a dictatorship under General Metaxas. As the conflict in western Europe developed, Greece found itself drawn into the vortex of international politics in spite of a strong desire to remain neutral.

Although a traditional bond of friendship with Great Britain as well as the presence of the British Mediterranean Fleet strongly influenced the Greeks in favor of that country, there was also a healthy respect for the military might of Germany. However, after the Italian declaration of war against Great Britain in 1940, relations between Greece and the Axis nations rapidly deteriorated and a number of Italian acts of aggression against Greek shipping aroused the ire of the Greek people. When, on 27 October 1940, Mussolini issued an ultimatum announcing his intention to occupy portions of Greece, neither the government nor the people were in the mood to acquiesce.

One of the benefits of the Metaxas dictatorship had been the build-up of a well integrated national army. When Italian forces invaded Greece from Albania on 28 October, Metaxas immediately threw his small but well trained army against the numerically stronger invader. Although superior in armament as well as numbers, Mussolini's legions were no match for the thoroughly aroused Greeks. By early 1941, the Greek forces had occupied nearly a third of Albania and had inflicted losses of over 100,000 on the Italians.

Despite ethnical, political, cultural, and economic differences, the Greeks had immediately achieved a high degree of national unity when the Italians attacked. Supply problems had, however, plagued the army and food and ammunition were critically short throughout the entire Albanian Campaign. By the spring of 1941, the Italians had been able to bring up strong reinforcements. The Greek advance stalled and the Italians launched an offensive. Although the Greeks were able to contain the attack, their resources of men and materiel were strained to the utmost.

When Bulgaria joined the Axis Pact on 1 March 1941, the route south was cleared for a German invasion of Greece. That such an invasion would come was a foregone conclusion, as the move was dictated not only by strategic requirements of the German campaign in Africa but also by the necessity for Hitler to rescue his Italian partner from the unenviable position in which his Greek fiasco had placed him. As German intentions became clear, in accordance with Britain's agreement guaranteeing the territorial integrity of Greece, some 58,000 British troops were rushed to bolster Greek defenses.

The German Army, using strong mechanized forces, crossed the Greek border from Bulgaria on 6 April 1941, and with the speed typical of panzer tactics moved rapidly south. In spite of its successes against the Italians, the already over-extended Greek Army did not have the resources to combat the German military machine.

Metaxas, the strong man of Greece, might have delayed the German juggernaut by rallying the nation but he had, perhaps fortunately for him, died in January while the Greeks were still gaining victories over the Italians in Albania. The Greek general staff as well as the field generals were, for the most part, completely overawed by evidences of German invincibility, and by the time the Germans struck the Greek Army was already psychologically defeated.

By 9 April, Salonika had fallen and the Greek forces in eastern Macedonia and Thrace were isolated. A wave of defeatism engulfed the Greek command and the task of conducting the final resistance to the German drive fell mainly on the British Expeditionary Force. While British forces in the Mount Olympus and Larisa area made futile attempts to stem the advancing panzer divisions, another German armored column cut behind the Greek divisions in Albania, forcing their capitulation on 20 April. The surrender of this important element of the Greek armed forces assured the success of Hitler's blitzkrieg. With the northern part of the country overrun and the two principal components of its army defeated, on 21 April the Greek Government informed the British that resistance was no longer possible. The British fell back

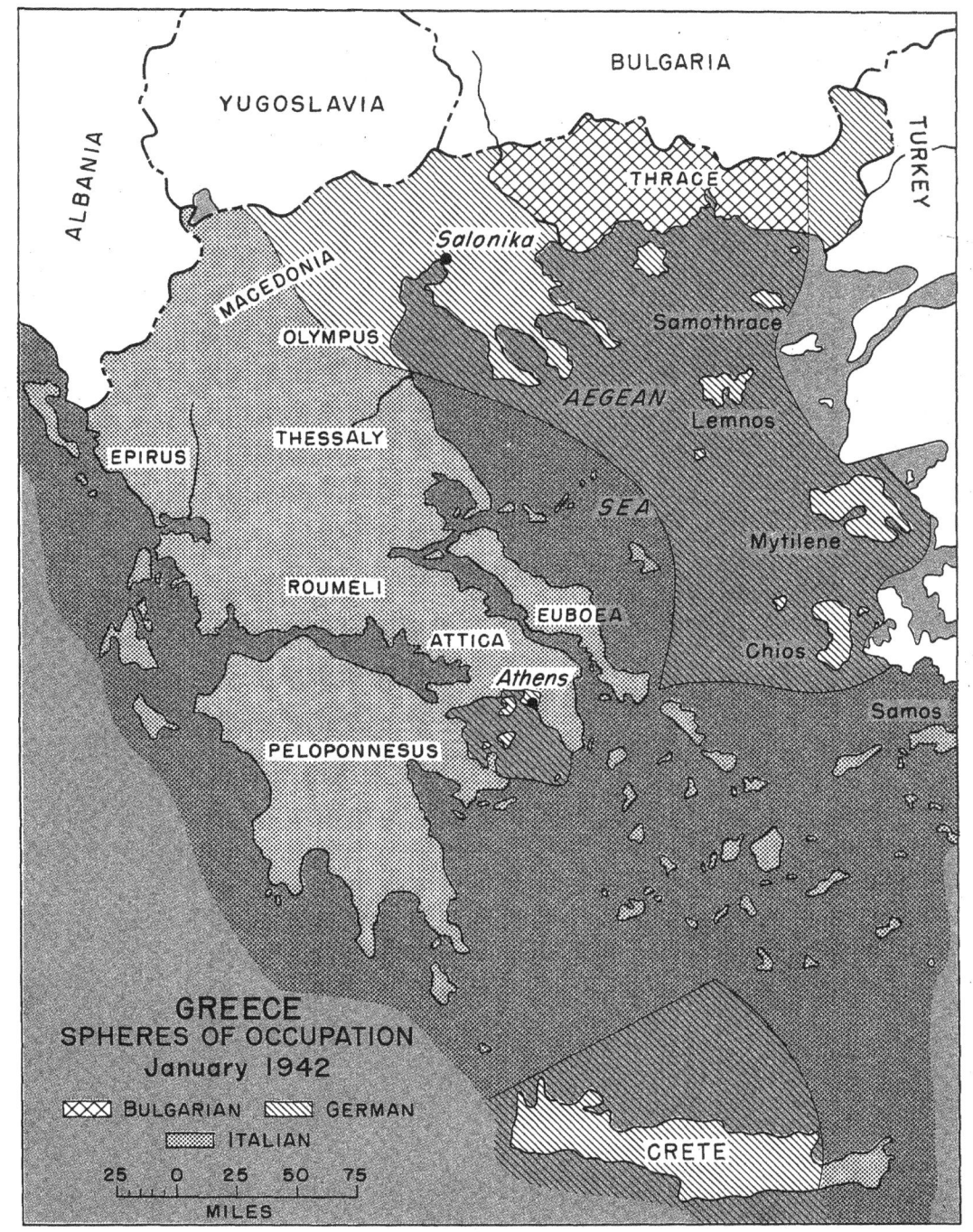

Map No. 1

to the south and within the next few days about 42,000 British troops and a large number of Greeks were rapidly evacuated from ports in Attica and the Peloponnesus.

The king, the prime minister, and most of the important government officials fled Greece. Koryzis, who had succeeded Metaxas, died by his own hand on 20 April and his successor, Tsouderis, accompanied King George in his flight. A Government-in-Exile was first established on Crete and then, after the fall of that island, in Cairo.

On 27 April, just three weeks after crossing the northern border, German units entered Athens and, within a matter of days, set up a puppet government. The new government was under the ineffectual leadership of General Tsolakoglou, who had disobeyed orders by signing an armistice with the Germans and Italians on 23 April.

Following its successes in Greece proper, the German Army moved swiftly against Crete and, by the first of June, had gained possession of that strategically important island.

## Greece in Defeat

One of Hitler's principal purposes in seizing Greece had been to open a line of communications with north Africa. With this objective accomplished and with the campaign against the Soviet Union imminent, the German Army Command could not afford to tie up large numbers of first class fighting men in occupation duties. Following the conquest of Crete, most of the combat units were withdrawn and the occupation of Greece was turned over to Hitler's Axis partners. The Germans held only a few key points: Athens-Piraeus, Salonika and a large area to the north and west; a strip of Thrace along the Turkish border; the western portion of Crete; and a few of the more important Aegean islands. The balance of the country was occupied by the Italians, with the exception of some parts of Thrace and eastern Macedonia which Bulgaria was permitted to annex.

The only railway from Salonika to Athens was utilized by the Germans to supply their forces in Africa and Crete. Shipments of food to the cities virtually ceased and the Greek people, who were already existing at a bare subsistence level, were reduced to starvation. The food shortage in Athens was particularly acute and the Axis occupiers did little to alleviate the situation.

The inability of the Italians to direct the puppet government properly soon became apparent and the breakdown of effective governmental controls added to the misery of the Greek people. A blackmarket developed, inflation set in, and the spectre of starvation continued to stalk the land. The condition of the masses in the cities was particularly pitiable and the sight of people dying of starvation in the streets became commonplace.

The death of Metaxas, swiftly followed by the German invasion, and the subsequent flight into exile of king and government had stunned the nation and left it leaderless. Since the Metaxas regime had suppressed not only the Communists, but also many outspoken liberal and republican leaders, the flight of the government had created a political vacuum. The ineffectual puppet government was collaborationist and most Greeks wanted no part of it. With the monarchist leaders in exile, left behind were only little known liberal politicians and military leaders of widely divergent political views and the Communist Party which, having been suppressed for four years, had developed no leaders of national prominence.

As the people recovered from the shock of their stunning defeat, the desire to offer resistance to the Axis became widespread. For the first few months, however, there was little indication of the rise of a resistance. The political differences which had disappeared at the time of the Italian attack again divided the people and no universally popular leader had risen. Although army officers and politicians formed cliques which held innumerable clandestine gatherings to discuss and plan resistance to the Axis occupiers, political views and personal convictions as to methods to be employed differed so radically that there was little agreement among individuals or groups. Among most of the plotters there was general agreement only in that they were opposed to the return of the monarchy and a possible dictatorship. Discussions between embryo resistance organizations invariably ended in acrimonious debates on the type of government to be established when, as, and if Greece was liberated. Even the most enthusiastic of patriots grew discouraged with the seeming impossibility of forming a unified resistance movement which would act now and argue politics later.[2]

Chaotic conditions and a lack of leadership created a situation made to order for the Greek Communist Party and its leaders were not long in recognizing their opportunity.

## Development of the Resistance Movement

The Greek resistance first started in the larger cities and, by the fall of 1941, evidence of organized underground activity was clearly discernible in Athens and Salonika. Although a number of resistance groups eventually became active, the Communist Party was the first political organization to recover from the shock of defeat and was, therefore, responsible for inspiring or directing most of the early resistance action.

The Greek Communist Party (Kommunistikon Komma Ellados), known as KKE, had been developing an efficient underground organization since the time of its suppression by Metaxas in 1936. As the liberal politicians and military men continued to hold their interminable conferences and secret meetings, the Communists were improving their organization within the larger cities and expanding into the country districts.

To direct the resistance movement, KKE followed the established Communist technique of acting through a front organization and was responsible for forming the National Liberation Front (Ethnikon Apeleftherotikon Metsopon), or EAM. Aligned with KKE to form the resistance organization were the Union of Popular Democracy, the United Socialist Party, the Socialist Party of Greece, and the Agrarian Party, all oriented well to the left although not Communisitic. Although theoretically nonpartisan, with KKE only one of several member parties, EAM was developed and built on the old Communist underground network and had a Communist-dominated central direction committee in Athens.

After its organization on 27 September 1941, one of EAM's first efforts was to organize a propaganda service and within a short time a host of bulletins and news-sheets were being printed in Athens and Salonika for circulation throughout the country. Slogans were painted on walls and, as EAM advertised its existence, its membership grew with great rapidity.

The over-all EAM structure was built on the hundreds of small villages in which Communist cells had been established during the Metaxas regime. In each village the secretary of the local EAM organization was designated as the Ipefthinos, or "responsible one." In most cases, it was the Ipefthinos who had organized the local communist cell and who had been instrumental in recruiting the villagers to the cause of KKE and, later, EAM. Regardless of what other village officials there might be, the Ipefthinos was the ultimate authority and it was through the "responsible ones" that EAM was able, eventually, to maintain control over large areas of Greece.

Not all who supported EAM were Communists or Communist sympathizers. In fact, few of the rank and file were aware of that organization's bond with Communism.[4] EAM offered an opportunity to oppose the Axis occupiers and this was the main concern of most of its members.

Another front utilized by KKE was the Workers National Liberation Front, or EEAM, the only organization really representative of Greek labor. EEAM was strongly infiltrated, if not completely controlled by KKE which directed the labor organization in a highly successful campaign of resistance throughout the occupation. Starting in the fall of 1941, slow-downs, public demonstrations, and sabotage were almost continual occurrences in Athens and other centers in which a large labor population existed. Later, in the summer of 1943, strikes organized by EEAM were largely responsible for frustrating attempts to conscript Greeks for labor in Germany.

Toward the end of 1941 and in early 1942, other resistance organizations developed and became active in gathering intelligence, disseminating propaganda, and conducting sabotage. All of these later organizations were formed by more conservative elements than the supporters of EAM, but none of them ever achieved the prominence or numerical strength of the Communist organization.[5]

## Appearance of Overt Resistance

With its roots well planted in the cities, the resistance movement spread to the mountains where its manifestation was to be overt rather than clandestine. In place of the work stoppages, propaganda activities, and intelligence gathering of the cities the people of the country were encouraged to take up arms in open guerrilla warfare.

It is generally conceded that certain conditions must be fulfilled before a guerrilla movement can develop. By the end of 1941, all the prerequisites necessary for the start of armed resistance were present:

Favorable Terrain: The predominately mountainous character of the Greek peninsula offered ideal terrain for guerrilla operations. In the rocky crags, almost completely inaccessible to motorized conventional forces, lightly armed bands could move without difficulty. The few roads which connected the principal towns and villages often wound through narrow gorges which could be easily blocked or in which a conventional force could be ambushed.

Tradition of Violence: The entire history of Greece had been a record of almost constant external and internal warfare, civil strife, and resistance of oppression. Guerrilla warfare was a tradition that dated back even further than the struggles against the Turks and to many it had continued to be a way of life -- the mountains of Greece had probably never been entirely free of bandits.[6] The mentality, background, and actual training of many of the Greek mountain people were admirably suited to the conduct of active resistance.

Civilian Support: The tradition of violence and a common hatred of the enemy insured the willingness of the people to support as well as participate in a guerrilla movement. Although the low standard of living might limit the quantities of food or other material that the populace could supply, the needs of the guerrillas would not be great. The fact that economic standards were low also meant that there was little to lose and this, too, would have an important bearing on popular willingness to support the guerrilla movement. In addition, the impossibility of the occupying powers adequately policing the many mountain villages would make it possible for the people to support the guerrillas with some degree of impunity.

Motivation: The Greek Army had already decisively beaten the Italians and the people of Greece strongly resented having their country occupied by Mussolini's troops. Their hatred of the Italians, already well developed, had become intensified. The fact that Bulgaria had not merely occupied the northern area, but had annexed it and begun colonization, did nothing to endear that traditional enemy to the Greeks.

In addition to patriotism and a hatred of the enemy, other standard guerrilla motives were present: opportunity for personal gain, self-aggrandizement and, in the case of the Communists, a political ideology violently opposed to that of the fascist occupiers.

Chance of Success: While, in 1941 and early 1942, there could not have appeared to be much chance of an Allied success, when one has little to lose, the chance for success need not be great. The Greeks had long respected British might and the Communists had faith in the ultimate victory of the USSR. These two influences, combined with the entry of the United States into the war, may well have offset any doubts of eventual success for the Allied cause. In addition, the Greeks had little fear of the Italians or respect for their fighting ability.

Effective Leadership: Although no leaders of national prominence had yet appeared, there was no lack of local leaders capable of forming small armed bands. Many of these were former members of the Greek Army and some were bandit chiefs with bands already in being. The resistance organizations, particularly EAM, were also active in encouraging the formation of bands and seeking to enlist them as supporters.

Outside Support: Support from outside sources is not absolutely necessary to the start of a guerrilla movement, it is only required to insure its growth and success. There should, of course, be some possibility of receiving such support and the Greeks were reasonably certain that it would be forthcoming. British agents had been active in Athens and promises of help had been made. With a long seacoast and a large seafaring population, possessing many fishing boats, communication with the outside world posed no serious problem. The guerrillas could be reasonably sure that Allied assistance would be forthcoming.

With the primary prerequisites satisfied and with the resistance organizations, particularly EAM, active in arousing the people of the mountain districts, the rise of a guerrilla movement was natural -- in fact, it would have been strange if it had not developed. Although there was little overt activity during 1941, by the spring of 1942 a viable guerrilla movement was in being.

The Guerrilla Organizations[7]

Although representatives of EAM may well have been instrumental in encouraging the formation of many guerrilla bands, for the most part the Greek guerrilla movement was a spontaneous local phenomenon. It was a popular rising in which small bands developed almost simultaneously throughout the mountain districts during early 1942. The Greek people referred to the guerrillas as andartes -- the name given to the irregular forces that fought the Turks in 1821.

The independent bands had little knowledge of the resistance organizations of the cities and few of their members had joined as a result of political loyalties. Later, the resistance organizations, desiring to sponsor military arms, dispatched leaders into the field who were successful in combining the many small bands into larger, more effective forces. The emissaries of the resistance groups also brought politics to the guerrilla movement. Within a comparatively short time the great majority of guerrilla bands found themselves aligned with one of two opposing political camps: Communist and anti-Communist.

There was little co-ordinated action among groups opposed to EAM as they were split into their own political camps: monarchist, republican, or socialist; each distrusting the eventual political aims of the others. Only among the EAM-sponsored bands was there cohesion and singleness of purpose. Its tight-knit organization, combined with the advantage of having been first in the field, was largely responsible for the leftist group outstripping all rivals.

### ELAS

The Greek People's Liberation Army (Ellinikos Laikos Apeleftheretikos Stratos) or ELAS, was formed as the military arm of EAM.[8] Like its parent organization, ELAS was theoretically nonpartisan but, also like EAM, it was under the effective control of KKE. As in EAM, the majority of the rank and file members of ELAS were not necessarily Communists; only its leadership was of the left.

Although efforts to promote a guerrilla movement began in late 1941 and bands were in existence in early 1942, EAM did not announce the organization of ELAS until April 1942. Thereafter, its growth was rapid. Soon after its formation, ELAS inaugurated a campaign to control the entire Greek guerrilla movement by bringing all independent bands under its leadership. That this campaign was eventually successful was due to ELAS' well-established and tightly controlled organization as well as to the fact that its methods were completely ruthless. Failing to integrate a band through persuasion, ELAS would surround it with a superior force and offer a choice of joining up or being wiped out. Under such pressure, most of the small, local bands quickly accepted service under the ELAS banner. Later, larger forces were also attacked and either integrated or eliminated. To justify the extermination of other guerrilla bands, ELAS offered the argument, "Those who are not with us are against us." All rivals were accused of collaborating and with collaborators hated even more intensely than the enemy, it was not difficult to build up enthusiasm for the elimination of "collaborationist" bands.

The ELAS andarte groups, at least the larger units, were distinguished by having tripartite commands: a military commander, a capetan, and a political advisor. Although right from the beginning, many of the military commanders were junior reserve officers or former noncommissioned officers of the Greek Army, ELAS was originally shunned by most of the higher ranking Greek Army officers. Later, when ELAS definitely indicated that it had become the dominant guerrilla organization, a number of respected and conservative officers lent their services. In time, ELAS enlisted the services of 16 generals, 34 colonels, and 1,500 other commissioned officers from the pre-war Greek Army.[9]

The military commander of the ELAS andarte units was limited to the planning, organization, and direction of purely military operations. In general, the capetan was the popular leader, quite frequently the man who had originally formed the band. Usually he commanded the loyalty and had the confidence of the individual andarte as well as the local civilian populace. In this position and with this following, the capetan was the logical man to be responsible for propaganda, morale, recruiting, administration, and the requisitioning of supplies from the villagers. He frequently acted as assistant or second in command to the military commander who, assigned by ELAS or EAM headquarters, often had little familiarity with the members of the bands or the local community. The third member of the command team, the political advisor, was a thoroughly indoctrinated Communist charged with responsibility for seeing that the party line was followed. He was also vitally concerned with the political indoctrination of the individual andartes.

The capetan having been, in most cases, the man chosen by EAM to organize a particular locality was either a Communist or a man politically acceptable to KKE. Between the two, the capetan and the political advisor, the military commander was effectively prevented from deviating from the policies adopted by KKE and passed to ELAS through EAM.

Not only was the military commander kept under the thumb of KKE but the civilian community was also closely controlled. As the area controlled by EAM/ELAS grew larger, the National Civil Guard, or EP, was organized to maintain public order and exercise a measure of control over anti-EAM elements. Directing the efforts of EP was OPLA (Units for the Protection of the People's Struggle), an organization seldom visible to the public eye but which combined for EAM the functions of Gestapo and SS.[10]

### EDES

Only one other guerrilla force of major importance developed in Greece. Colonel Napoleon Zervas, a former Greek Army officer, raised a sizable force which operated principally in the Epirus region. His organization developed as an outgrowth of a resistance movement formed in Athens on 9 September 1941, called the Greek Democratic National League (Ellinikos Dhimocraitikos Ethnikos Sindhesimos) and was popularly known by its initials -- EDES. The titular head of EDES was the highly respected General Plastiras. However, since he had been in exile in France for some years and remained there throughout World War II, his participation in the EDES resistance movement was minimal. Both Zervas and Plastiras were strongly republican and, although rightists, were against the monarchy.[11]

With General Plastiras absent, policy decisions of the Athens resistance organization were made by a committee of which Zervas was originally a leading member. On 23 July 1942, seeking to engage in more direct action, General Zervas had returned to his native district of Epirus and begun the formation of a guerrilla force which grew rapidly. As in the case of ELAS <u>andartes</u>, the individual band members did not necessarily subscribe to the republican politics of Zervas and the other EDES leaders, they merely went along with the strongest organization in the area. However, because of its moderate political aims and the reputation of Plastiras and other leaders, EDES originally attracted a greater number of professional soldiers than did ELAS.

Eventually, the field EDES broke with the Athens EDES over a question of politics. Although the original resistance organization had been strongly republican and antimonarchist in sentiment, several pronouncements by Zervas appeared to favor the return of King George II. This break made little difference in the operations of the EDES field force as Zervas, having been a senior member of the political EDES as well as guerrilla leader, had never been subject to any great amount of control from Athens.

The headquarters and main strength of EDES remained in Epirus throughout the war but small EDES forces operated briefly in western Thessaly and in the Peloponnesus.

### EKKA

Another Athens resistance organization, known as the National and Social Liberation (Ethniki Kai Koinoniki Apeleftherosis), also generally referred to by its initials -- EKKA, sponsored a guerrilla force which took the field some time after ELAS and EDES.

EKKA was socialistic -- slightly to the left of EDES, but well to the right of EAM. Although it was formed soon after the occupation of Greece, it was late in getting a force into the field. It was not until early 1943 that Colonel Dimitrios Psaros succeeded in recruiting a number of men from his old regiment to form the EKKA guerrilla force. Operating in Roumeli, the native district of Colonel Psaros, the EKKA guerrillas may have numbered as many as one thousand at the height of its strength. The band eventually fell a victim to ELAS although the political organization in Athens continued to function after its field force was dispersed.

### Other Andarte Organizations

In the Peloponnesus, where EDES was never strong and ELAS was extremely weak originally, two related groups took the field during

1943. The National Organization of Officers, or EOA, was theoretically a resistance organization guiding the operations of a group of guerrilla bands, rather grandiosely known as the Greek Army, or ES. Actually, EOA was not only a control group since, in addition to the ES bands, a number of guerrilla units operated under the name of EOA. Led by officers of the recently demobilized Greek Army, both EOA and ES were strongly rightist in politics and supported the return of the monarchy.

The lives of these monarchist guerrilla organizations were extremely short. Having begun operations in the early summer of 1943, in October all EOA and ES bands were wiped out by ELAS which had experienced a phenomenal growth in the Peloponnesus. The bands and their leaders were scattered, some joining the puppet government's Security Battalions and some transferring their allegiance to ELAS. Discouraged by a situation in which Greek fought Greek instead of Germans, the great majority simply returned to their homes to await further developments.

George Papandreou, later prime minister, was instrumental in forming an Athens resistance group which was known simply by the initials AAA. In late 1942, General Pangalos and Major Tsigantes, AAA's principal military guides, persuaded Colonel Stefano Sarafis to go to central Thessaly and attempt to unify independent guerrilla bands under AAA. Colonel Sarafis met with some success in gaining followers but his guerrilla movement died in infancy. In March 1943, he was captured by ELAS guerrillas and, after being a prisoner for some time, was persuaded to join that organization. Like EKKA, AAA continued as a political organization but, after the defection of Sarafis, it never succeeded in establishing a field force.

A resistance organization, first called YVE and later known as PAO, was formed in Salonika in the early days of the occupation. Although it early established an intelligence net which passed information of some value to the British Middle East Command and received substantial sums of gold in return, it was late in forming a military arm. Between March and July 1943, PAO organized a force numbering approximately a thousand men in the mountains of eastern Macedonia. Organized in some twelve bands, the PAO guerrillas conducted operations as much against ELAS as against the Germans. ELAS accused PAO of collaboration, took action against its bands, and by October 1943 succeeded in eliminating them. ELAS' accusation of collaborating may have had some basis in fact as there is evidence that remnants of the PAO bands worked closely with the Germans in counterguerrilla operations against ELAS in the spring of 1944.[12]

Not all the guerrilla forces were sponsored or organized by resistance organizations. A number of bands maintained an independent status throughout the Greek conflict but they seldom achieved any real importance and made little contribution to the war effort. An exception to this was a sizable force headed by a man known as Anton Tsaous.[13] Starting operations in eastern Macedonia and Greek Thrace toward the end of 1943, his bands were known as Capetanioi until he later developed the more formal designation of Greek Nationalist Guerrilla Bands. Tsaous' bands received considerable British support and fought the Germans, Bulgarians, and ELAS with equal enthusiasm.

A last group which should be mentioned -- if only for humorous relief -- was organized and led by a man who called himself Athos Roumeliotis, a pseudonym derived from the Roumeli area which he claimed to control. At one time an ELAS band leader, he broke with that organization and withdrew to a remote part of the Pindus Mountains in early 1943. Roumeliotis' activities seem to have been confined to acting as a local chieftain or headman within his small zone of influence, where he performed marriages and collected taxes. From time to time he issued rather pompous pronouncements and enthusiastically offered to enter into negotiations with ELAS, EDES, and EKKA. He made little or no actual contribution to the resistance and when, in August 1943, his force was dissipated by ELAS his passing was little noted by the Greeks, the British, or the Germans.

## Outside Influences on the Development of the Guerrilla Movement

Friendly or allied powers outside an occupied country seldom find it advisable to lend support to a guerrilla movement until it has achieved some significant success, is well established, and its course can be predicted with reasonable accuracy. In late 1942, however, the British situation was unusual and, because of the exceptional circumstances, the Greek guerrilla movement received outside aid and encouragement before it had proved itself worthy of support.

British plans for the El Alamein counteroffensive against Rommel's Afrika Korps called for the disruption of German supply lines to Africa. Since the Athens-Salonika railroad was a vital link in Rommel's supply chain, its disruption was of paramount importance to the British Middle East Command. Unable to achieve its destruction by sea or air, during October the Middle East Command parachuted twelve liaison officers into the mountains of Greece with the mission of organizing guerrilla support for the task. With the help of both EDES and ELAS bands, the British Liaison Officers (BLO's) succeeded in destroying a key railroad viaduct and were thereafter retained in Greece as the nucleus of a British Military Mission (BMM) assigned to the Greek guerrilla forces.

Builders of morale as well as suppliers of much needed weapons and ammunition, the BMM encouraged the rapid growth of the guerrilla movement and directed the operations of the andarte bands in furtherance of the strategy of the Middle East Command.[14]

Guerrilla Leadership

It is recognized that guerrilla leaders are generally men of rebellious nature who have spent their lives resisting constituted authority. In addition, the more successful of them have frequently been unsavory characters whose reputations, if not already established, were achieved as a result of their guerrilla activities.

The few men who rose to national prominence as leaders of the Greek guerrilla movement did not deviate from the accepted pattern. All were rebels to a greater or less degree and all had records of consistent defiance of the established government of Greece. The majority had either a questionable past or, during the resistance, acted in a manner which cast doubt upon their personal integrity.

The backgrounds and characters of the most prominent Greek guerrilla leaders are best known from the comments of the BLO's, who worked closely with them. In accepting British judgment, however, it is well to be warned that their opinions are possibly biased by an understandable antipathy toward Communism, in general, and EAM/ELAS, in particular.

Strangely enough, a man who rose to one of the highest positions in ELAS was forced into that organization virtually at pistol point. The story of Colonel Stefano Sarafis not only gives some insight into the character of a prominent guerrilla leader, but also illustrates one ELAS method for gaining the services of respected military men.[15]

Colonel Sarafis had an excellent military record and was respected by many Athens liberals. He was antimonarchist, having been exiled for his participation in the attempted republican coup of 1935. At the start of the Greco-Italian war, he was permitted to return to Greece, but, although he volunteered, was not accepted for military duty. Soon after the beginning of the occupation, Sarafis met on numerous occasions with various groups of military leaders and liberal politicians who were seeking to organize resistance movements. In Athens, he was approached by EAM and tentatively agreed to join, then withdrew, presumably because of its radical doctrine. On two occasions, Sarafis was jailed and interrogated by the occupation authorities but was released for lack of evidence of subversive activity. Upon gaining his freedom the second time, he began an association with the newly formed AAA resistance organization. Early in 1943, AAA sent Colonel Sarafis to Thessaly to unify guerrilla bands in the Trikkala area.

Having enlisted two sizable bands under the AAA banner, he traveled to Epirus to discuss co-operation with EDES. At a meeting with General

Zervas and Colonel Myers, chief of the BMM, plans were laid for a loose confederation of AAA in Thessaly, EDES in Epirus, and EKKA in Roumeli, a region to the south of Epirus and Thessaly. Under the terms of the agreement, in addition to paying one British pound per month for the upkeep of each guerrilla, the British would undertake to provide all three organizations with weapons, ammunition, clothing, and other supplies.

Returning to Thessaly, Sarafis discovered that there had been serious friction between his AAA bands and ELAS. While attempting to settle the differences, on 1 March he was captured by an ELAS band and accused of collaborating with the enemy. As a prisoner he was moved from one ELAS area to another and, in spite of the fact that he could not have felt any great liking for his captors, he was tremendously impressed by the tight-knit ELAS organization. Eventually, he became convinced that only through the strong organization of EAM/ELAS could an effective resistance be developed. When, after having been a prisoner for some five weeks, he was offered his freedom he immediately expressed his desire to serve with ELAS. Subsequently, he was offered the military command of all ELAS guerrilla forces and accepted with alacrity. After returning to Athens to report his decision to AAA, he donned his old Greek Army uniform with some pride and returned to take over his new duties.

Although Sarafis claims that his choice was made of his own free will and volition, the British were of the opinion that his acceptance of service with ELAS was strongly influenced by the fact that the alternative would have been death.[16]

The recruitment of Sarafis was a most astute move on the part of EAM/ELAS as it lent an air of greater respectability to their organization and, as a result of his acceptance of command, a number of other former Greek Army officers were induced to join ELAS. There is little to indicate that as commander-in-chief of ELAS, General Sarafis had any great authority or that he was kept fully informed by EAM, his <u>capetan</u>, or his political advisor.[17] He was useful to KKE, EAM, and ELAS as a front man of considerable respectability and, as a former Greek Army officer, it was thought that he would be an excellent agent to deal with the BMM. In this latter department, Sarafis must have been somewhat of a disappointment as his later relations with the British mission were far from cordial.

In describing his first meeting with Colonel Stafano Sarafis, the chief of BMM said:

> I should have paid more attention to his rather weak chin and evasive, watery blue eyes than to his aquiline features, military moustache and straight, close-cropped, dark, but slightly greying hair, which gave him superficially quite a determined appearance. Upright, of average build and height, between forty and fifty years of age and dressed in a dilapidated knickerbocker suit, my first impression of him was that he looked like a reliable soldier.[18]

According to Sarafis' own account, his principal activities appear to have been the making of tours of inspection and delivering of speeches to enthusiastically cheering crowds in each town or village through which he passed. This indication that the people were unanimously and wholeheartedly behind EAM/ELAS still further confirmed Sarafis in the rightness of his decision. It never seems to have occurred to him that the demonstrations were a little too well organized to have been completely spontaneous. On his trips he was almost invariably accompanied by a reliable Communist guide, while Aris Veloukhiotis, his _capetan_ associate, remained with ELAS fighting units and did considerably more troop leading than did the military commander.

Many guerrilla leaders, particularly those of ELAS, adopted pseudonyms, either to hide an unsavory past or to make it difficult for the enemy to identify them and take reprisals against their families. As a security measure, the BLO's also adopted the practice of using their given names rather than their surnames.

One guerrilla leader who adopted a _nom de guerre_ was Aris Veloukhiotis, whose real name was Athanasios Klaras, and who was referred to throughout Greece simply as Aris.[19] According to C. M. Woodhouse, Aris was the fighting genius of ELAS, rivalled only by Zervas in the whole guerrilla movement of Greece.[20] Unfortunately for the Allied cause, Aris' genius was not so apparent to the Germans for, with a few notable exceptions, most of his fighting was against other Greeks.

Aris did not have to be forced to join ELAS at pistol point. As a matter of fact, there is evidence to indicate that he formed one of the first guerrilla bands, offered its services to EAM, and his band thereafter became the nucleus from which ELAS developed.[21]

Denys Hamson, one of the original BLO's, came to know Aris as well, if not better, than the other members of the mission. His description of Aris is, therefore, undoubtedly accurate:

> In those moments I gathered a little of what he was -- no respector of persons, a hard, cold man. I suppose he was the most ruthless man I have ever met, the most cold-blooded, the cruellest. He was an ex-schoolteacher, sentenced in Greece

for homosexual offenses and trained in the Moscow School of Communists, an intelligent, able man with no heart, without human pity, an excellent psychologist, a fanatical leader of men. Later, when I came to know him better, I had no doubt that after one of our all-day drinking sessions in the most friendly atmosphere, he would have literally flayed me alive if it had suited his purpose. He was still a pederast and it was noticeable that for a henchman he always had a good-looking, rosy-cheeked youngster. He became an almost legendary figure -- he was very brave physically -- and he met a violent death in 1945 when a follower of his killed him and his boy companion with a hand grenade.[22]

Aris habitually wore a black uniform and cossack cap which was decorated with a skull and crossbones insignia. As a bodyguard he had enlisted a group of fanatics who emulated their leader's dress and attempted to match him in courage and cruelty. Throughout Greece, Aris and his private guard were famed and feared for their tortures and killings.[23]

Among the chief guerrilla leaders, General Napoleon Zervas was undoubtedly the British favorite. In their writings, BLO's speak of his cheerful disposition, his winning personality, and his willingness to co-operate with the BMM and the Middle East Command.[24] Allegations that Zervas played both ends against the middle and had dealings with collaborators as well as the German occupation forces are either refuted by his supporters as being Communist propaganda or admitted and condoned as examples of his shrewdness in fooling the Germans.[25]

Prior to his association with EDES, Zervas had a very checkered career. He had long been an ardent republican, having fought with Veniselos in 1917, on the side of the Allies and against King Constantine. In 1926, as a colonel in the Greek Army, he had been a staunch supporter of General Pangalos, the republican dictator, but broke with him to follow General Kondylis, another republican. Under the royalist dictatorship of Metaxas he had been imprisoned for a time.[26] At one period, after being purged from the army, he had been a well-known professional gambler in Athens.[27]

Zervas was a skilled and effective leader, gaining the respect of both the British and Germans for his military prowess. In spite of the fact that he was criticized by some of his followers for his refusal to delegate authority to his lower echelon commanders, he later placed many of his bands under the direct orders of the BLO's.[28]

Another guerrilla leader whose star burned brightly for a time was Colonel Dimitrios Psaros of EKKA. Although he was successful in forming a sizable force, his career as a guerrilla leader lasted less than a year and could scarcely be considered as an over-all success. He, like Zervas and Sarafis, had been associated with republican causes and had actively opposed the monarchy. The BLO's admired him for his personal integrity and Colonel Myers, in recording his impressions of Psaros, noted that he was too honest for the intrigues of resistance politics.[29] Colonel Psaros was also highly regarded by General Sarafis, who once offered him command of all ELAS and EKKA forces in Roumeli.[30] Later, when Psaros had been killed and his EKKA guerrilla force destroyed by ELAS, his character was summed up by Woodhouse in a eulogistic phrase, ". . . the only guerrilla commander who was what the British Army calls an officer and a gentleman."[31]

In addition to the principal leaders, there were many hundreds of lesser guerrilla chiefs who displayed leadership ability and achieved some local fame. There was no lack of trained military leadership in Greece, the army had not been destroyed or imprisoned and many former officers were willing and anxious to carry on the war against the Axis. From the beginning, most of Zervas' band leaders were former officers and, eventually, many ELAS units had military commanders who were former officers or NCO's of the Greek Army.[32]

Considering its radical political doctrines, brutal methods, and ruthless extermination of other guerrilla forces, the question of how ELAS gained the support of so many normally conservative army officers naturally arises. To understand these officers' association with ELAS, it should be recalled that its Communist control was carefully disguised. The other parties in the EAM coalition made it acceptable and its domination by KKE was not apparent at the guerrilla band level. In addition, KKE's ultimate aim of imposing Communism on Greece through the agency of EAM/ELAS was not advertised to the uninitiated. Later, after the officer had joined ELAS, if he became cognizant of the real situation, it was too late -- he was prisoner of the system. No matter how distasteful the Communist tactics and ideology may have been, he could not escape. The punishment for defection was death.[33]

The experience of one Greek officer who espoused the ELAS cause with the hope of reforming it is cited by one of the British Liaison Officers who served with the Greek guerrillas:

> Kalabalikis, the commander of IX Division, a member of the Popular Democratic Union (ELD), had joined ELAS in 1943 with the hope shared by many other of serving his country within the limits that ELAS might allow and at the same time of lessening the increasingly political aspect of the organization. He was a

short, cheerful, bespectacled man, who did his utmost as an able military commander to carry out operations against the enemy. But he trod a razor's edge of existence between the military needs of the situation and the political threats and supervision of his politikos. In the end, a few weeks after liberation, he was sent down to Athens by the Mission /Allied Military Mission/ for his own safety.[34]

Another reason that army officers joined ELAS is more obvious; if an officer wished to fight for the liberation of his country, ELAS was possibly the only guerrilla organization available to him. In time, ELAS became the dominant guerrilla force in Greece and controlled some four-fifths of the country. Only a few bands operated independently in Macedonia, while Zervas and his EDES force were restricted to the small region of Epirus. Even if an officer wished to join Zervas or the Macedonian bands, he normally would have to pass through ELAS-controlled territory and such movement was denied those who did not carry passes issued by EAM/ELAS. Neither organization was in the habit of providing passes to those who wished to take service with their rivals.

## Guerrilla Headquarters

The headquarters of the small andarte bands were simple affairs, frequently being contained entirely under the hat of the leader. Even when a band had grown to respectable size, rosters of members, location of supply depots, and other headquarters data was not committed to paper. Such records, if captured by the enemy, would be disastrous for the individual and his family as well as to the band.

Although there was tremendous variation, depending on the size, location, and situation, the physical equipment of a headquarters often consisted only of a shack, tent, or cave in which the leader and one or two men who comprised his staff could meet. Occasionally, another facility would house whatever communications equipment the headquarters might possess -- if the band had been lucky, a portable radio or field telephone. Since headquarters equipment was held to an absolute minimum and few records were kept, when displacement was required the commander and his staff had little to do but take off. None of the bulky impedimenta of a conventional headquarters delayed their departure or impeded their progress.

When a guerrilla organization was being formed, headquarters was often set up in a town where suitable buildings existed or where some form of communications was available. Later, when an actual fighting group had been recruited and organized, security precautions usually required the movement of the guerrilla headquarters into a mountain village or wooded campsite less accessible to the enemy. Whenever possible, the headquarters was situated on high ground which permitted observation of the surrounding countryside while offering concealment to the guerrillas.

Villages were frequently used for winter quarters of bands and headquarters, as were the summer mountain homes of wealthy townspeople from the plains. In some areas the guerrillas established winter quarters in the rude shelters which sheepherding families occupied during the summer months when the herds were grazing in the highlands.

As soon as a headquarters had been compromised, either through enemy reconnaissance or by an informer, it would be moved. Often, displacements were made in great haste with an enemy punitive force hot on the heels of the last man to leave. The general area of the next headquarters was usually known in advance and the andartes made their way to the new location individually or in small groups. Later, headquarters establishments became more complex, particularly for the larger guerrilla units. General Sarafis notes that the movement of ELAS headquarters in late 1943 required the use of ten trucks as well as a mounted escort.[35]

## Supply and Headquarters Security

Supply and security problems are not necessarily related, but for the Greek andartes they were closely linked and the solution of one problem also solved the other.

The andartes lived off the land, depending on food donated, purchased, or requisitioned from the villagers. The Greek mountain villages being small and extremely poor, it was impossible for any one village to support a large body of andartes. As a consequence, in order to be supported by the civilian population it was necessary for the larger forces to decentralize. Small bands were assigned to locations, generally in or near a village, in a radius of several miles around the headquarters.[36]

This decentralization not only removed an impossible burden of support from any one village, but also established an outpost line which provided security for the headquarters, making it almost impossible for an enemy force to approach undetected. The dispersion of the bands also denied the enemy any really profitable targets and it was rare that a counterguerrilla force was able to capture more than one or two isolated guerrilla bands.

The outposted bands did not constitute the entire security net. A large proportion of the civilian community was active in obtaining and passing information to the andartes. Inhabitants of the larger towns and cities, in which enemy troops were garrisoned, passed on word of troop movements and preparations. News of an enemy force moving into the mountains would be quickly relayed by villagers. The many wandering shepherds alertly watching their flocks were just as alertly watching the roads and, together with the townspeople and villagers, formed an important adjunct to the security net.

Although a headquarters or village in which there were important caches of arms, ammunition, or food would sometimes be defended temporarily while the supplies were being moved, the andartes seldom attempted to conduct a static defense of a village or headquarters site. Generally, to avoid reprisals, the guerrillas and most of the male inhabitants of the village would move out ahead of a punitive force and seek the safety of nearby mountains.[37]

Food was a continual problem to the andartes and the villagers who supported them, even though the demands of the andartes were not great -- bread, goat's milk cheese, some fruit or olives, and an occasional sheep or goat took care of dietary requirements. Many bands had their own flocks of sheep and goats which traveled with them, needing only corn meal or fruit from the villagers.

For military supplies the guerrillas originally depended on thefts from enemy depots or the ambushing of convoys. Clothing shortages were frequently overcome by stripping enemy dead. Air drops by the British Middle East Command eventually provided many military supplies -- permitting the standardization of weapons and even providing uniforms for large numbers of andartes, particularly EDES. In addition, quantities of British gold given to the guerrilla organizations permitted the purchase of amny items of sustenance and was even used to buy arms and ammunition on the blackmarket which flourished in the garrisoned towns. In the fall of 1943, the surrender of the Italians resulted in the andartes acquiring much valuable equipment, including horses, trucks, and heavy weapons. ELAS received a far greater share of the captured Italian war material than did EDES, as the Pinerolo Division and the Aosta Cavalry Regiment surrendered both men and equipment to ELAS general headquarters in Thessaly. No major Italian units surrendered to EDES.

The andartes were chronically short of medical supplies but this was a situation quite easily remedied. With complete disregard for the customs and usages of war, the ambush of a lightly guarded hospital convoy effectively solved the medical supply problem. The Germans complained bitterly about the guerrillas' disregard for the Red Cross and cited frequent examples of the ambush of unarmed medical convoys in which all ambulances were wrecked and all patients killed.[38]

### Evacuation of Wounded and Medical Care

Guerrilla bands usually made every effort to remove their dead and wounded from the scene of battle; a practice dictated by a number of vital considerations. Although some bands may have been motivated by a praiseworthy and humanitarian desire to save wounded comrades from torture and death at enemy hands, the primary reason for evacuating the wounded was to prevent their interrogation by the enemy. Removal of dead and wounded also forestalled assessment of guerilla losses as well as identification of units or individuals, with the possibility of subsequent reprisals against families and friends.

If the battle casualty survived the ordeal of being dragged up and down precipitous mountain paths and was placed in the care of friendly villagers he might recover. Unfortunately for the sick or wounded andarte, there were few doctors in the mountains and about the most the sufferer could hope for would be the application of crude, but often effective, home remedies. Attempts were sometimes made to get doctors from the larger towns and cities or to secretly take sick or wounded guerrillas to the doctors. However, since the enemy controlled most of the urban areas, both these practices were fraught with danger to all concerned: the doctor, his family, the patient, and those who brought him to town.

In general, the wounded Greek guerrilla had little more chance for survival than did the soldier of the 18th Century. The efficacy of the country remedies and the hardiness of the Greek peasant's constitution is attested by the fact that many apparently hopeless cases survived and regained good health.[39]

## Communications and Security

Judged by conventional military standards, the communications systems of the Greek <u>andartes</u> were primitive in the extreme. There were few telegraph lines or telephones in the mountain areas and the amount of signal equipment that had been inherited from the disbanded Greek Army was negligible. While the <u>andartes</u> made valiant efforts to establish efficient communications nets, the lack of radio, telephone and telegraphic equipment did not handicap them to the extent that it would a conventional force. Guerrilla operations normally being of independent nature there is little need of the co-ordination and constant contact required for conventional operations. In addition, the mobile nature of guerrilla tactics makes the possession of elaborate or cumbersome signal equipment most impractical.

In spite of a paucity of modern signal equipment, the guerrillas of Greece built up a remarkably efficient communications system. Existing wire lines were utilized to fullest capacity and the large number of radios which were supplied by the British were augmented by those which the guerrillas constructed from parts of civilian sets or captured equipment. All manner of expedients were used to pass warnings to guerrilla bands of the approach of enemy forces: church bells, engine whistles, or even the arrangement of laundry hung on lines or spread on the grass.

In the final analysis, however, it was not electrical means or special expedients on which the guerrillas principally relied, it was the courier. Members of guerrilla bands or local villagers, who knew every path and short-cut through the rugged mountains, bypassed enemy patrols and carried news or maintained liaison between bands and their headquarters. The Germans as well as the members of the Allied Military

Mission were continually amazed at the speed with which news traveled through the Greek mountains.[40] In describing a trip which he took through remote areas of Macedonia, Major Jerry Wines who commanded the U.S. Army mission to the Greek guerrillas, writes: "There was seldom a telephone or telegraph line in this mountain country yet, despite the apparent lack of communications between villages, we were always expected. Runners, of course, was the answer . . ."[41]

The communications net of the guerrillas was principally useful for security purposes and, as an early warning system, it was most successful. It was seldom possible for an enemy patrol or counterguerrilla force to completely surprise a guerrilla band or force. It was just as well, perhaps, that the andartes were not dependent upon wire or radio communications for operational direction as signal security was almost entirely lacking. Due to lack of adequate security training, radio and telephone messages were generally sent in the clear with no attempt being made to use codes. German monitoring and wire-tapping was constant and their intelligence agencies were usually well advised of the location and situation of guerrilla headquarters. Telephone lines installed by the andartes were seldom hidden or camouflaged; frequently being laid on the ground or strung from bushes and trees. Counterguerrilla forces soon learned that the following of a wire would lead them to a guerrilla hideout or supply cache of a headquarters, even though they didn't find the guerrillas still there.

The BLO's brought radios and operators with them on their mission to the Greek mountains and additional radios were received through air drops. Each area in which a BMM team was stationed had a radio and operators at the district headquarters. These installations were not, however, used for internal communications but only for signalling SOE Cairo; although the latter headquarters frequently relayed messages to or from intelligence agents and resistance organizations in Athens.

## Recruiting

At the inception of the guerrilla movement, all members of the Greek andarte bands were volunteers, many being former soldiers who required little inducement to continue to fight against the despised Italians. In general, these original volunteers constituted the hard core of the andarte organizations and often became unit leaders as the movement expanded.

Although recruiters and organizers were active throughout Greece, propaganda and the publicizing of operational successes proved to be among the most effective means of encouraging men to join the bands. Largely as a result of Zervas' EDES force participating in the destruction of the Gorgopotamos viaduct, his force increased from a strength of 98 in September 1942, to approximately 600 by the first part of 1943. In March, EDES strength rose to 4,000.[42] During the same period and for much the same reasons, ELAS also experienced a phenomenal growth.

Not all the andarte recruits were former soldiers or mature men; the thrill and excitement of a guerrilla's life appealed strongly to the young and youths of fourteen or fifteen were common in the andarte ranks. Even younger boys were frequently used as messengers and lookouts.

Joining a guerrilla band was not just a simple matter of a prospective recruit presenting himself at the headquarters of the nearest band. To ensure that volunteers were not spies or enemy agents, the new recruit had to be vouched for by some person or persons known to the band leader. Resistance organizations frequently supplied this certification in addition to conducting recruiting activities. In the case of ELAS, which had a widespread organization, the volunteer had to obtain a recommendation from the local EAM committee. Armed with the proper credentials, the applicant would be accepted -- provided a weapon was available for him.[43]

One of the factors that discouraged recruitment in the early days of the guerrilla movement was lack of weapons. The inability of the bands to supply arms not only made men reluctant to join but also caused band leaders to discourage the enlistment of those who came unarmed. The receipt of weapons from the British made it possible to accept and arm many additional recruits.

Those joining the Greek guerrilla bands were motivated by all the usual stimuli: such as patriotism, hate, fear, self-aggrandizement, and desire for adventure. One well-informed writer, however, ascribes the desire to escape the drudgery of peasant life as a compelling motive for enlistment with the andartes:

> In actual fact, a soldier in ELAS lived a good deal better than did the ordinary peasant of Greece, and did not have to work with the same drudging toil. He further had the psychological exhileration of believing himself a hero and the true descendant of the robber klefti who had fought in the War of Independence and were enshrined in the Greek national tradition. Under the circumstances, many a peasant's son found himself irresistibly attracted to the guerrilla life; and an overabundant peasant population made recruitment easy. Fewer came

> from the towns; life was relatively comfortable there, and EAM had other work for townsmen, organizing strikes and serving as propagandists among the more illiterate peasants.[44]

Although McNeill mentions ELAS specifically, EDES, EKKA, and the small independent bands had much the same appeal for the Greek peasant.

German and Italian counterguerrilla measures served still further to augment the guerrilla forces. Reprisals which were calculated to cow the civilian population had, more often than not, the reverse effect. The burning of villages and the indiscriminate shooting of civilians engendered strong feelings of hate and a thirst for revenge that resulted in many of the survivors not only joining the *andartes* but also becoming its most fanatical members.[45]

Guerrilla sympathizers in the villages frequently constituted a part-time guerrilla force which could be called on to participate in specific operations in which considerable strength was required. Such reserves not only provided temporary strength increases but, when detected by the enemy the part-time guerrilla had no other recourse than to flee to the hills and become a full-time resistance fighter. In 1943, German attempts to conscript Greeks for labor in Germany forced many men into the hills to join the *andarte* bands.

When the flow of volunteers dried up or failed to total the numbers desired by the larger guerrilla organizations, systems of conscription were developed. Because it controlled a large part of the country, conscription was more widely used by ELAS than any other guerrilla organization. The guerrilla auxiliary or resistance organization within the towns and villages, acting as arbitrary selective service boards, selected "volunteers" for service with the local bands.

Conscripted men were not invariably the most ardent of resistance fighters and, in spite of the severe penalties which might be incurred, desertions and defections to other bands or to the Germans were not uncommon.

The ELAS method of forced recruitment of entire bands has already been discussed. Although such practices were not entirely unknown to other guerrilla organizations, the group impressment method was most extensively employed by ELAS. Like the conscripts, the morale and loyalty of the impressed groups was questionable.

As the German evacuation of Greece became imminent and the day of liberation approached, the flow of volunteers to the andartes increased by leaps and bounds. Those who had held off, following a wait and see policy, were anxious to jump on the band wagon once the issue was no longer in doubt. Since ELAS, at that time, held some four-fifths of the country it was only natural that the great majority of the latecomers gravitated to its ranks. With their ultimate goal of instituting a Communist regime in Greece now clearly in view and anxious to build up its strength at any cost, ELAS seldom inquired too closely into the antecedents of the new recruits. Many of these were prominent political and military leaders and not a few had also been known collaborators. Apparently volunteering for service, however late in the day, was accepted by ELAS as evidence of true repentance. In October 1944, ELAS claimed a total strength of nearly 50,000 -- an increase of 20,000 over the 30,000 men claimed in the spring of the same year.

## Weapons

It was not manpower but lack of weapons that limited the growth and size of the Greek guerrilla bands. Weaponless men were understandably reluctant to engage in guerrilla sorties and band leaders were not anxious to recruit more men than could be armed. There were, of course, a great many weapons in the hands of the mountain villagers. Many of the soldiers of the Greek Army had never been disarmed after the surrender -- when news of the collapse of formal Greek resistance had reached them, many small units had merely disbanded and the men had returned to their homes carrying their arms. After the bands began operating, additional weapons were obtained by capturing or stealing them from the Italians.

Ammunition was in short supply, as the returning soldiers could carry only a limited number of rounds. Fortunately, Italian cartridges fitted the Mannlicher rifle with which the Greek Army had been equipped, and thefts from Italian stocks as well as the stripping of killed or captured Italians helped solve the ammunition problem.[46]

In addition to Greek and Italian army rifles, the <u>andartes</u> carried other weapons of all sorts and descriptions, including fowling pieces, antique muzzle loaders, and ancient pistols. Most carried knives as well as firearms.[47]

The first BLO's brought in a number of Sten guns and these automatic weapons were highly prized by the <u>andartes</u>. Later, air drops of standard British rifles were made in some quantity -- eventually enough to entirely rearm the EDES and EKKA forces and to materially improve the armament of ELAS.

The guerrillas had virtually no heavy weapons until the surrender of the Italians resulted in ELAS acquiring some mountain guns in addition to large numbers of rifles. Still later, when EDES seized a sector along the west coast of Greece, the British shipped in many mountain guns.[48]

## Training and Discipline

The training of the Greek <u>andarte</u> was often rather haphazard, even in those bands which were sufficiently well organized to conduct a planned training program. Lack of time, equipment, or facilities frequently precluded giving a recruit any training before he was required to take an active part in a combat operation. Actually the original members of the bands gained their knowledge and experience by trial and error. It was only after the guerrilla movement had developed to the point that a paramilitary organization was established that definite programs for training recruits were inaugurated.

The time devoted to training varied greatly depending on the situation, the size of the band, and the background of the individual recruit. Former members of the Greek armed forces received as little as four or five days training, while recruits without previous military experience sometimes were given as much as five to six weeks of instruction.[49] Training for both types of recruit was based on Greek Army regulations but was confined primarily to the handling of weapons, demolitions, security, and instruction in guerrilla tactics. Much of the work consisted of training for night operations, including mine-laying in total darkness. The recruit without any military background was also instructed in the rudiments of discipline. In ELAS, much time was devoted to political indoctrination, both in the first few weeks and as a continuing project. In late 1943, ELAS established an officer training school, graduating its first class of 136 sublieutenants in September. Graduation ceremonies were attended by several British Liaison Officers. In October, a second and larger class began training. Later, the students also served as an elite guard for ELAS General Headquarters.

Physical conditioning, while important, was not normally considered as a vital part of training since the recruit from the mountains had usually led an active life -- lack of transportation facilities having accustomed him to walking long distances over the most rugged of terrain.

Training in weapons was severely handicapped by the shortage of ammunition and, as a consequence, guerrilla marksmanship was generally poor. Fire discipline was virtually nonexistent and guerrillas frequently opened fire prematurely or fired on targets at impossible ranges. The BLO's early noted that men armed with automatic weapons kept their fingers glued to the triggers and often fired entire magazines where short bursts would have sufficed or been even more effective. Certainly, a more controlled use of ammunition would have helped to conserve the always inadequate supply. Lack of fire control was also responsible for the failure of ambushes and for many <u>andartes</u> being shot by their own comrades.

W. Stanley Moss, a BLO who was dropped into Macedonia in late 1944, recounts a conversation between two British commandos of the

Raiding Support Regiment which was then operating in Greece. Although not the best historical evidence, the conversation is reprinted here as an indication of the average British officer's opinion of guerrilla marksmanship and fire discipline.

"Any casualties?" asked Bertie.

"Four," the major replied. "Three <u>andartes</u>, shot by the <u>andartes</u>, and one of our chaps, also shot by the <u>andartes</u>."

"What about the enemy?"

"One or two, perhaps."

"I doubt it," said the lieutenant. "The Greeks were too busy shooting each other."[50]

Some specialized training was given selected groups of <u>andartes</u> by British and American Liaison Officers, particularly in the field of demolitions. Here again, the program was handicapped by shortages of explosives for training purposes. Since demolitions work was too dangerous to permit "on the job" training, throughout the entire period of the resistance the liaison personnel were required to perform most of the demolitions tasks themselves -- particularly where major targets were involved.

Possibly the chronic shortage of demolitions was attributable, at least in part, to rather generous estimates of requirements for demolitions jobs. Captain Arthur Edmonds, one of the first British officers to be dropped into Greece gives evidence of the profligate use of explosives in his description of the blowing of the Gorgopotamos viaduct:

> Invariably when planning a demolition we calculated the minimum charges required, then, reckoning that once we reached the target we must be certain there were no hitches, we would double the charge to allow for them being faultily placed in the haste of the operation. If explosive was available we might even double up those charges.
>
> When lecturing the Haifa sabotage school on this operation later, I staggered them by telling them the quantity we used. The same result could have been achieved with one-tenth the total charge, but of course we were in the dark as to the size of the bridge members until we reached the target.[51]

To professional military men, such as General Sarafis and some of the liaison officers, the average andarte band must have appeared to be an unruly mob. The lack of uniforms, failure to salute, or inability to fall in according to height and march in a military manner would be, to an old soldier, indications of a lack of discipline. Such criticism, however, implies a failure of the critic to understand that the disciplinary standards of guerrillas differ from those of conventional forces. The guerrilla shines no shoes or brass and has little use for the "spit and polish" discipline of regular troops. However, as far as control by leaders and obedience to orders was concerned, the Greek andarte was generally well disciplined.

With a situation in which all bands were without the law and with many bands composed of lawless elements, discipline was, of necessity, strict. Owing to the mobile nature of guerrilla operations, imprisonment was not a practical solution to disciplinary problems. Punishments such as reduction in rank, loss of a prized weapon for a time, or often just a blow or reprimand from the guilty man's superior were among the most common for less important offenses. Severe beatings or death were not unusual penalties for major transgressions. Aris once shot one of his men for stealing a chicken and General Zervas punished several of his officers for failure to properly control their men.[52]

The discipline imposed by the guerrilla leader was not confined to the members of his band but extended also to the civilian community. One instance of Aris' methods of dealing with lawless elements in the mountains is furnished by the chief of the BMM:

> Meanwhile Aris disappeared. I learned afterwards that he had gone to a neighboring village, where a case of cattle-thieving had been reported to him. He had the culprit stripped and publicly beaten in the village square by the newest recruit, a mere boy. It was in this way that he "blooded" his new adherents. He had then pulled out his revolver and shot the guilty man. Thus was law maintained by Aris in the mountains of Roumeli at that time.[53]

Other leaders, besides Aris and Zervas, were equally efficient in dealing with depradations by their own men or by civilians in the areas under their control.

Civilian Support

Although the larger guerrilla organizations were sponsored by resistance organizations in the big cities, they seldom received anything more valuable than advice or political guidance from their urban sponsors. Occasionally, the resistance headquarters directed recruits to the fighting units or furnished funds which British agents had provided but, for the most part, they contributed only words. Since most of the members of the urban resistance groups were concerned primarily with postwar plans and were not familiar with the guerrilla situation or conditions in the mountains, their advice was seldom of practical value. Except for ELAS, which EAM kept under tight control, the advisory services of the resistance organizations were seldom requested and even less frequently followed.

The real support of the Greek andartes came from the people of the small mountain villages. There, strong elements of sypathizers and supporters, often comprising whole villages or districts, gave freely of what little they had. In some cases these supporters had a more or less formal association with the resistance organizations -- especially when EAM had organized the district -- but generally they were just the relations, friends, or former neighbors of the individual andartes. These supporters, which constituted a guerrilla auxiliary, were seldom dignified by any title, but were known only as sympathizers or "reliable" people. Certain locations were referred to as reliable villages or districts, meaning that the people were loyal to the local guerrillas. Despite a lack of formal recognition, the villagers' bonds with the andartes were very close, and without such backing the guerrilla bands of Greece could never have existed.

Leading at best a hand-to-mouth existence, the Greek peasant had little food to spare for the andartes and voluntary contributions, however freely given in some areas, seldom produced the quantities required by the guerrilla forces. EDES requisitioned some items of subsistence from the villages of Epirus but, being plentifully supplied with British gold, Zervas' force purchased much of its food either from the peasants or on the blackmarket. ELAS, backed by the well-organized EAM, instituted a unified system of taxation which was aimed at spreading the support burden over the widest possible base.

The EAM/ELAS tax collection agency was ETA (Epimeletes tou Andarte) which enforced a schedule of taxation based on the peasant's ability to pay. Taxes, generally collected in kind, were progressive. No tax being levied on the minimum quantity deemed necessary for subsistance. Thereafter, on a scale which rose sharply in relation to the amount of excess produce, a percentage was taken of the taxpayer's grain, olives, tobacco, fruit, fish, or livestock.

About 20 percent of taxes collected were earmarked for support of local EAM activities and civil administration, with the balance being delivered to ELAS depots. Although the system was designed to fairly apportion the burden of supporting ELAS, emergencies and the exigencies of the situation often necessitated the seizure of far greater amounts than were called for under the basic plan. Where an individual or entire village was suspected of being anti-EAM or failed to co-operate with ELAS, all produce as well as livestock might be forfeit.

The principal function of the villagers was to provide logistic and intelligence services to the guerrillas. The auxiliary, those most closely associated with the local bands, arranged for supplies of food, often carrying it for long distances into the guerrillas' mountain hideouts. Supporting services also included medical care with the village doctors, where such existed, treating sick and wounded guerrillas who were later hidden in or near villages while being nursed back to health.

As an intelligence net, the people of the villages were invaluable. Their services in providing the <u>andartes</u> with security information and timely warnings saved many a band from surprise attack and possible extinction.

Transport service was another major contribution of the villagers. Where they possessed mules, they formed trains to carry radios, demolitions, ammunition, or the containers dropped by the supply planes of the British. Where no mules were available, the people themselves carried the supplies and, as the men generally considered such work beneath their dignity, much of the lugging of heavy burdens was done by women.[54]

During 1943, both EDES and ELAS developed an armed reserve composed of those who, for physical or other reasons, could not engage in full-time andarte activities. The Reserve served many useful purposes: it performed communications and liaison duties; provided guards or security detachments; and constituted a force which could be mustered for emergencies.

EAM also formed the United Panhellenic Youth Organization (Eniaia Panellinios Organosis Neolaias). Popularly known as EPON, the youth movement was encouraged for propaganda purposes. Major Jerry Wines has recorded having seen an EPON girls' military unit in Macedonia:

> . . . among the marchers was a platoon of uniformed girls, outfitted in battle dress, with rifles and bandoliers of ammunition. It was the first and only women's unit I saw among the Greek andartes, and I am of the opinion that this was a showpiece hastily assembled to greet two of Tito's Jugoslav women guerrillas who were in Pendalofon at this time on some Red mission.[55]

General Sarafis, however, claims that EPON girl units took an active part in ELAS operations and mentions specifically that a girls' company performed well in the last ELAS campaign against EDES.[56] Although there is no doubt that members of EPON actively assisted the guerrilla bands in many ways, the principal reason for its establishment was to swell the numbers of EAM and gain control of the youth of Greece for Communism. Neither EDES nor any other resistance or guerrilla organization ever approached the high level of civilian organization achieved by EAM/ELAS.

The Ipefthinos was the key figure in organizing civilian support and maintaining liaison with the local ELAS bands. He checked the identification papers of strangers coming to, or passing through his village and vouched for local men who wished to join the andartes. The Ipefthinos was also the one to whom the andartes looked to provide them with mules and guides.[57]

The Greek Orthodox Church, always strongly nationalistic, was particularly active in support of the resistance. At least six bishops supported EAM, while many monasteries and priests' homes sheltered guerrillas or cared for the wounded. The village priest was often the most energetic in rallying the people and stiffening the occasionally flagging morale. Together with the village mayor or Ipefthinos, the priest frequently formed the link between the local guerrilla leaders and the people. Although such service was unusual, priests sometimes accompanied the guerrillas and one actually led an EDES band.[58] In spite of its communistic ideology, EAM/ELAS never became publicly antireligious.

The people of the mountain country of Greece paid a heavy price for their assistance to the guerrillas. While the guerrillas were fleeing to safety after executing an ambush or act of sabotage, the enemy took action against the more static civilian population. Always the villages in the immediate neighborhood of any major sabotage operation or attack on troops were the objects of enemy reprisal. Houses were burned, hostages were taken, and often large numbers of civilians were shot. Reprisal action by the Italians was severe, but they lacked the thoroughness of the Germans. When the latter took over responsibility for counterguerrilla operations in 1943, they were not content with burning out the stone houses which might later be rebuilt, but added dynamite to the torch and totally demolished town after town and village after village. In addition, they were less selective and more promiscuous in their shooting of civilian hostages.

Eventually, when the people learned that the <u>andartes</u> were gathering for a major operation, they precluded personal reprisal action by evacuating their homes and fleeing to the safety of the mountains. Although the reprisals of the occupation forces made hundreds of thousands of people homeless, the Greek peasant bore it all with great fortitude. John Mulgan, a British Liaison Officer who came to Greece in the summer of 1943, pays tribute to the Greek peasant:

> The real heroes of the Greek war of resistance were the common people of the hills. It was on them, with their bitter, uncomplaining endurance, that the German terror broke. They produced no traitors. We moved freely among them and were guided by them into German-held villages by night without fear. They never surrendered or compromised, and as a result the Germans kept five divisions guarding Greece all through the war. The Greek people paid a terrible and disproportionate price for this resistance.[59]

## CHAPTER II

## EARLY OPERATIONS AND LIAISON WITH THE BRITISH
## (1942)

### The Occupation

For many years, relations between Germany and Greece had been most friendly. Greek rulers had been of Germanic blood and, during World War I, the Greek people had been sharply divided between pro-Ally and pro-German factions of the government. In the years immediately preceding World War II, German economic ties with Greece had gradually been strengthened to the point that Germany had become the principal market for Greek exports and had, in turn, been the foremost supplier of manufactured imports.[1]

The treatment of the Greek Army, at the conclusion of the German invasion of 1941, had been extremely generous -- instead of being placed in prison camps or detention centers, the Greek soldiers had merely been disarmed and permitted to return to their homes.

Bearing in mind the close ties between Germany and Greece as well as their generous treatment of the Greek Army, the Germans felt that their presence in the land would not be violently opposed by the Greek people. German military writers, in discussing the occupation of Greece, have stated that relationships with the Greeks were pleasant at first and intimate that the resistance movement would never have developed had the Germans remained as the sole occupation power. It was, they have implied, the act of turning the administration of the country over to others that was responsible for arousing the people -- not only against the Italians and Bulgarians, but also against the Germans who had made it possible for the despised Italians to control most of Greece.[2]

As proof that the Greeks bore them no ill-will, the Germans point out that there were virtually no guerrilla operations undertaken against German forces during 1941 and 1942 -- that the Italians and Bulgarians bore the brunt of all overt resistance action.[3] By suggesting that no guerrilla actions were directed against the Germans because the Greeks bore them no ill-will, German writers ignore the obvious. There were very few guerrilla bands in operation as early as 1941 and, in 1942 in the areas where the great preponderance of guerrilla bands had their inception and development, there were no Germans. The remote mountain areas that spawned the andartes were within the Italian and Bulgarian zones and the resistance fighters struck at the only available targets.

In Salonika, the one large area occupied by German troops, guerrilla operations were initiated soon after the occupation began. North of Salonika, in an area garrisoned by the 164th Infantry Division, there were acts of sabotage and terrorism as early as October 1941. The German division effected prompt and severe retaliation. In seven towns in the vicinity of Salonika, between 23 and 25 October, troops of the 164th Division rounded up all males between the ages of 16 and 60 and executed them -- a total of 416 men and boys. The seven villages were razed and the women and children resettled in other villages.[4] A group of six Moscow-trained Bulgarian Communists who had been parachuted into the area to encourage and lead a resistance, were quickly rounded up and just as quickly dispatched. Such prompt and drastic action appeared to discourage the flowering of the guerrilla movement in that region. Although resistance groups continued to function clandestinely within the city of Salonika, overt action against the German forces in that part of the country did not develop again for many months.

There is little doubt that regardless of what nation or group of nations had occupied the country, resistance and guerrilla movements would have developed. General Wilhelm Speidel, Military Governor of Greece during much of the occupation, was probably more familiar with the over-all situation than any of his military or civilian colleagues. In his analysis of the Greek resistance movements he states, ". . . any occupying force in any country will ever remain alien, and no matter how good its intentions may be, will make itself unpopular, if not hated."[5]

## Louros Gorge Ambush

While in a formative stage, with the guerrilla bands still small and unco-ordinated, their activities were necessarily restricted to thefts from enemy depots, cutting and stealing of telephone wire, waylaying of weak patrols, or sniping at the occupants of isolated outposts. It was not until October of 1942 that a guerrilla operation of major importance was undertaken.[6]

The only north-south highway in western Greece runs from Albania through the Pindus Mountains to Agrinion. There it turns east and, following along the northern shore of the Gulf of Corinth, leads to Athens. Since the British Navy was still a potent factor in the lower Aegean and Mediterranean Seas, the Italians were denied the use of the seaways in supplying their forces in Greece. The north-south highway, their only supply line to western Greece and the shortest land route to Athens, was heavily traveled by their convoys. Cities along the route were strongly garrisoned; two of the main points being Ioannina, principal city of Epirus, and Arta, about fifty miles to the south.

When Colonel Zervas, in the summer of 1942, had begun the formation of his EDES bands in southern Epirus, he had immediately realized that the disruption of supply arteries would seriously handicap the Italians. The Ioannina and Arta garrisons were far too strong to be attacked by his force of less than 100 men, but the convoys which regularly plied the main highway made ideal targets. Midway between the two strong points, where the highway crossed the Louros River, Zervas' scouts reported a perfect location for an ambush: a narrow, rocky defile which could be easily blocked and which could not be bypassed.

Reconnaissance revealed that Italian truck convoys regularly carried supplies from Ioannina to Arta, that trips were made always on the same day of the week and started practically at the same hour each time. Because there had been no subversive activity in the area the Italians had been lulled into a sense of false security; the convoys were lightly guarded and the same convoy pattern was invariably adopted.

Close observation of the convoy operations enable the EDES guerrillas to work out a virtually foolproof plan. The convoy would be halted in the defile, the guerrillas would fire from perfect cover, and the enemy would be powerless to retaliate. In addition, the high, rocky walls would deaden the noise of explosions and firing so that it could not be heard more than a short distance from the gorge.

Preparations for the ambush began at dawn on 23 October.[7] At the entrance to the defile, the bridge crossing the Louros River was heavily mined. About five hundred yards south of the bridge, mines planted across the roadway were carefully camouflaged. Taking no chances, Zervas' men not only employed pressure type detonators, but also hooked the mines to a cable detonator which would be used if the pressure fuses failed to detonate. Boulders, emplaced along the edge of the almost vertical cliffs, were so balanced that a slight amount of leverage would send them hurtling down to the road.

To cut off possible aid from the direction of Arta, a roadblock, covered by a small detachment of riflemen, was erected between the ambush site and the nearby town of Phillipia, a few miles north of Arta. Immediately above and below the Louros gorge, poles carrying telephone lines were sawed almost through so that a sharp tug on ropes tied to their tops would topple them and disrupt communications between Ioannina and Arta.

Along the cliffs between the two demolition points, the guerrillas prepared firing positions. Protected by outcroppings of the rocky escarpment, their two machine guns were emplaced in positions that afforded enfilading fire down the entire length of the gorge. Riflemen were dispersed along both sides of the road, armed with grenades as well as small arms. All preparations were completed before noon and Zervas' band, of less than a hundred men, lay in their positions throughout the afternoon.

Overenthusiastic resistance supporters in Ioannina nearly caused the ambush to fail. The previous night they had punctured tires on a number of the Italian convoy vehicles. During the morning vehicle line-up, in preparation for a noon departure, the sabotage was discovered and repairs effected. To anyone, other than the Italians, such sabotage activity might have suggested the exercise of extreme caution -- possibly the cancelling of the trip for that day. However, the Italian commander apparently decided that the punctures were isolated acts of vandalism, unconnected with any other resistance operation. The convoy was considered to be amply protected and, after making necessary repairs, the vehicles were ready to proceed -- only a few hours late.

Leaving Ioannina at 1600, the usual formation was assumed: the procession was led by a tank, closely followed by a truck with two mounted machine guns and a guard detachment. Next in line came the convoy commander's vehicle and, following that, nineteen trucks loaded with food, ammunition, and gasoline. On each truck, in addition to the driver, were two guards armed with automatic weapons. Bringing up the rear was a second tank.

One of the advantages of the ambush site was a high knob, just to the north, which permitted observation of the road for several miles in both directions. A lookout was posted on the knob to signal the approach of the convoy as well as to warn of reinforcements from either Ioannina or Arta.

Lying concealed, as the first vehicles crossed the bridge and entered the defile, the guerrillas held their fire. Upon reaching the mined section of the road, the lead tank detonated the mines and, careening out of control, plunged into the Louros River. Moments later the bridge was blown, just after the rear tank had passed over it, leaving the convoy completely bottled-up and at the mercy of the guerrilla band. Grenades and rifle fire pouring from the cliffs took a heavy toll of the Italians as they scrambled out of their immobilized trucks. Boulders crashing down from the heights added to the confusion and damage. The Italians panicked and rushed madly about seeking cover from the murderous fire. The bare highway, however, offered no protection and in a short time most of them were dead or badly wounded.

The rear tank, undamaged by the blowing of the bridge, directed its fire at the rocky battlements but, although some casualties were inflicted, the guerrillas were well protected and losses were light. A small group, approaching from a blind side, succeeded in placing and detonating a heavy explosive charge beneath the tank, completely destroying it and killing the entire crew. With this, an assault force of guerrillas rushed in to mop up the few Italians who remained alive.

Resistance being at an end, the guerrilla band turned its attention to the contents of the trucks. Mules, which had been held to the rear, were speedily brought up, loaded with captured supplies as well as wounded and dead guerrillas and started back to Zervas' headquarters. The trucks and supplies which the guerrillas were unable to take were soaked in gasoline and set afire. By nightfall, all was over and the last of the guerrillas had begun their withdrawal.

Concerned with the nonappearance of the convoy, the Italian command in Arta had discovered that the telephone line to Ioannina was dead. A motorcycle platoon was immediately dispatched north to check on the cause of the delay. The platoon soon returned with a report that it had run into a roadblock and had been fired on at a point about a mile and a half north of Phillipia. Unable to operate in the darkness and unaware of the size of the holding force, the platoon had withdrawn. It was too late then to organize a rescue and it was determined to wait until daylight before taking action.

A strong detachment, setting out at daybreak, found the roadblock abandoned and swiftly cleared the road. At the defile they came upon the evidence of the ambush -- burned and mutilated bodies, destroyed trucks and tanks. Of the guerrillas there was no sign. In characteristic fashion they had hit and run and, travelling throughout the night, were many miles from the scene of the ambush.

In an effort to find and punish the perpetrators of the attack, a strong Italian force combed the mountains between Ioannina and Arta. Although some contact was made and a number of skirmishes engaged in, for a period of over two weeks, the Italians were unable to destroy the band or even inflict serious losses.[8]

The Louros Gorge ambush was one of the most successful guerrilla raids in the Epirus area -- approximately 70 Italians had been killed and 23 vehicles, including 2 tanks, had been destroyed. Although it was the first major ambush along the north-south highway, it was by no means the last. Over the next year, similar operations were conducted at one location after another throughout Epirus. In their operations, the guerrillas were materially aided by the reluctance of the Italians to deviate from their established procedures. Although subsequent guerrilla attacks employed almost identical tactics and were consistently successful, the Italians' convoys continued to utilize the same convoy formation and follow set schedules for their supply runs.

Vehicular traffic from west to east was also constantly harassed. With the exception of the road that ran from Agrinion to Athens, there was only one other road that transversed Greece. Branching off from the north-south highway at Ioannina, the road ran eastward through the Pindus Mountains to Larisa, in eastern Thessaly. En route, the highway passed through the 5,000-foot Metsovon Pass, thence to Trikkala and on to Larisa where it joined the road from Salonika to Athens, the only north-south highway in eastern Greece.

Ambushes, roadblocks, destroyed bridges, and rockslides so frequently blocked the Ioannina-Larisa highway that its use was denied the Italians from late 1942 until the fall of 1943. Since the road ran from EDES territory through a large area controlled by ELAS, its blocking was a joint, though unco-ordinated endeavor.

Lacking cohesion and short of weapons, ammunition, and explosives, the <u>andarte</u> operations, for the most part, were restricted to minor sabotage and small-scale attacks prior to the arrival of British Liaison Officers in late 1942.

## Liaison with the British Middle East Command

There were, in Athens and Salonika, well-organized British intelligence nets. In addition, the resistance organizations had established propaganda bureaus which made it their business to advise the British agents on the progress of the resistance. Of course, not all the agents or propaganda disseminators were reliable and the British Middle East Command received some very optimistic reports on the size and potentialities of the guerrilla bands.

To supervise and direct the support of the Greek resistance, Special Operations Executive was established in Cairo which, for convenience, is referred to as SOE Cairo. Possibly because co-operating with resistance movements was a concept of war that was new, and perhaps slightly repugnant, to the British, the agency was never given the degree of power and autonomy it required for effective operation. In describing SOE Cairo, C. M. Woodhouse points up the difficulties under which that organization operated:

> It was responsible partly to the Ministry of Economic Warfare through its headquarters in London, partly to the Foreign Office through the diplomatic representatives of the latter, partly to the Commander-in-Chief for its operational activities. This triple responsibility was not defined as such on paper; but it was a reality and a source of confusion. More perplexing still was the internal confusion which can be shown by personal statistics. During four years of active existence, it was known under seven different names (besides that of SOE Cairo, which I have adopted as a portmanteau). Each change of name corresponded to a change of structure and nature; often slight, but always real and significant. During the same period there were eight different heads of the same organization, sometimes concurrently; three of them were civilians who did not entirely trust soldiers, and five were senior officers who did not entirely trust politicians or diplomats. The successive replacement of these men and their staffs did not always, though it did sometimes, coincide with those other rearrangements which peri-

odically changed the names of the whole organization. Able and conscientious individuals were therefore not always in a position to do their best as an organized whole.[9]

Further proving SOE Cairo's lack of continuity is the fact that four months after the first British Liaison Officers were parachuted into Greece, SOE Cairo was unable to find any record of their code names, which had been so carefully established before their departure for Greece.[10] Any agency so organized and operated could scarcely be expected to maintain a consistent policy and it is small wonder that there was often dissatisfaction among those with whom it dealt: the liaison officers, the guerrilla leaders, the Greek Government-in-Exile, and the press.[11]

With the Greek guerrilla movement still in its formative stage in the early fall of 1942, it might appear to the student of unconventional warfare that an attempt to enlist the aid of guerrillas was premature. The situation in the Middle East was, however, unusual and called for the adoption of unusual methods. The British forces in Africa, which had been pushed back into Egypt by Rommel's Afrika Korps, had been strengthened and by September 1942 a counteroffensive was in the making. Of vital importance to the El Alamein breakout plan was the disruption of German supply lines to Africa -- one of the most important of which was the main Greek rail line which ran from Salonika south to Athens-Piraeus which was estimated to be carrying 80 percent of Rommel's supplies.[12] SOE Cairo had received word that Colonel Zervas was operating in Epirus with about a hundred men and that a Major Aris, with Karalivanos as deputy, had formed a small guerrilla band in Thessaly.[13] Since

German airpower on the Greek mainland and surrounding islands precluded the bombardment of the vital railway by air or naval forces, the Middle East Command was forced to consider the possibility of guerrilla assistance.

A study of the single-track railroad showed several points that were extremely vulnerable to attack. Three viaducts -- Gorgopotamos, Asopos, and Papadia -- were all located within a ten-mile stretch of the rail line and all of them bridged deep, precipitous gorges. Should any one of them be destroyed, it would halt rail traffic for many weeks; a crucial period for both sides in the North African campaign. In an effort to effect the destruction of one of these structures, on 4 September a message was sent to a British agent in Athens asking that guerrilla bands in the area be urged to undertake the task.

A young Greek naval officer, named Koutsoyiannopoulos, who had fortunately adopted the code name of Prometheus, operated a secret radio in Athens and it was through him that SOE Cairo made contact with the guerrillas.[14] The request elicited the reply on 21 September that the guerrillas lacked necessary demolitions as well as qualified demolitions experts. The message added that to accomplish the task the British should drop at least ten parachutists, including demolitions experts and necessary explosives. A lawyer named Seferiades, with a group of followers, would meet the parachutists near Mount Giona, about twenty-five miles southwest of the three viaducts. The drop zone would be indicated by fires arranged in the shape of a cross. At the same time, the British were asked to drop an officer in the Epirus district to act as liaison between the EDES force of Colonel Zervas and the Middle East Command. Arrangements for signal fires and a reception committee were also made for this officer.

British Preparations to Effect Liaison[15]

SOE Cairo had no personnel trained in the complexities of guerrilla liaison. Further, it had no jump-qualified officers in its organization. As a consequence, it was necessary to cast around through the command and seek to discover some who had at least minimum qualifications to undertake the hazardous operation. As much by good luck as good management, SOE Cairo succeeded in recruiting a group of twelve men who, although not qualified in every respect, were better prepared than might be expected under the circumstances. Led by Colonel (later Brigadier) E. C. W. Myers, with Major (later Colonel) C. M. Woodhouse as second in command, a group of nine officers and three NCO radio technicians was assembled. All had received some parachute training and some had been members of commando outfits.

Three Liberator bombers, converted to permit the dropping of parachutists, were available to SOE Cairo for the operation. As each plane could accomodate four passengers, the group was divided into three self-sufficient teams of four men. Although one team was slated to drop initially into the Epirus territory of Zervas, all had the same mission -- to destroy one of the three viaducts. Each team was composed of a leader, a linguist, a demolitions expert, and a radio technician. All were to be dropped in uniform. Although it was hoped and expected that the teams would be able to unite and operate as a single unit for the viaduct operation, each team would be equipped to do the job alone. Necessary explosives, communications equipment, a number of automatic weapons, and funds in the form of British gold sovereigns would be dropped with each team.[16] As finally landed, the teams had the following composition:

Team No. 1 -- Colonel Myers, leader; Captain Denys Hamson, linguist (his commando training had also given him considerable knowledge of the use and handling of high explosives); Captain Tom Barnes, demolitions; and Sergeant Leonard Wilmot, radio technician.

Team No. 2 -- Major Woodhouse, leader; Captain Nat Barker, linguist (although his knowledge of Greek probably did not equal that of Woodhouse); Captain Arthur Edmonds, demolitions; and Sergeant Mike Chittis, radio technician.

Team No. 3 -- Major John Cook, leader; Lieutenant Themi Marinos, a Greek commissioned in the British Army, linguist; Lieutenant Inder Gill, demolitions; and Sergeant Douglas Phillips, radio technician.

From the moment of their first association, the use of all titles of rank as well as surnames was banned among the members of the liaison group. They were required to address each other only by their Christian names which were also to be their code designations for signal communications.

Influenced by information from Athens agents, the Middle East Command and SOE Cairo had formed a somewhat exaggerated estimate of the popular support of Zervas and the British believed that the guerrilla bands of Greece might all be unified and developed under

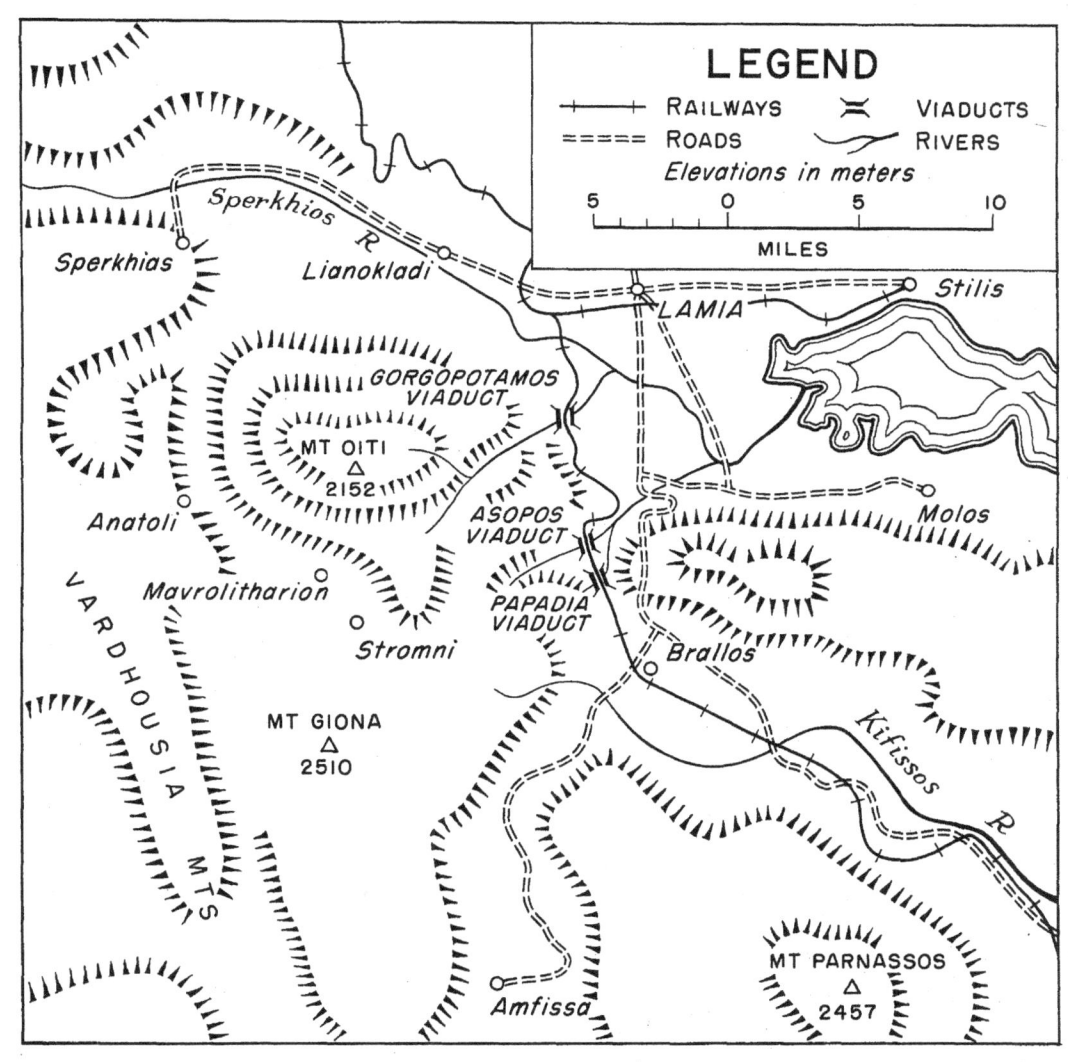

Map No. 2

Courtesy of the War History Branch,
Department of Internal Affairs,
New Zealand Government.

his leadership. For this reason, Woodhouse and his three companions were to be permanently attached to Zervas' headquarters. Woodhouse was particularly well fitted for the job. A young officer, he was in excellent physical condition and had spent the previous year working behind the enemy lines in Crete. He spoke fluent Greek and was well acquainted with the people and their country. The viaduct destruction operation was planned as a one-time shot; after accomplishing the mission all except Woodhouse and his party were to be evacuated from the west coast by submarine.

Entry of the Liaison Officers

Seferiades had suggested that the Mount Giona drop be made during the full-moon period between 28 September and 3 October. The signal fires would be lit every night during that period. On 28 September, just one week after SOE Cairo had received the request for the drop, the first attempt was made to infiltrate the teams. After circling over a large area of Greece and failing to see any fires arranged in a cross, the drop was cancelled. Two nights later, on the 30th, another try was made and Teams No. 1 and 2 accomplished their drops at points estimated to be near the prearranged locations. One plane, at least, had seen fires in the form of a triangle which might be construed as a drop-zone marking. The third team, not sighting any signal fires, dropped their supplies near the Mount Giona area and once more returned to Egypt. Just what the No. 3 team hoped to accomplish by dropping their supplies is not clear as they had no assurance that the other teams had dropped or that there would be anyone to receive them. After making several abortive attempts, Team No. 3 finally made its drop late in October.

Although the first two teams landed in extremely rugged mountain terrain no one was injured. Both teams and individuals were widely separated but, within a matter of hours, the members of each team had joined their respective leaders and, within a few days the two teams were reunited. Colonel Myers' team had landed near the small village of Karoutes, about ten miles south of their planned drop point near Mount Giona. Major Woodhouse and his team, which was supposed to have been dropped near Zervas' Epirus district, had landed many miles away; actually north and east of Team No. 1. Here it was received by a resistance group whose signal fires had been lit in expectation of a drop of explosives to be used in blowing a section of the Corinth Canal.

After each leader had assured himself of the safety and well-being of his teammates, his first concern was for the supply canisters which had been dropped immediately after the men. Colonel Myers was both angered and surprised to find that villagers in the vicinity had promptly appropriated his team's entire stock of food, weapons, and explosives. This situation was, however, straightened out by a local guerrilla leader named Karalivanos, who appeared while the British were attempting to recover their stolen supplies. By threatening the villagers with all sorts of dire consequences, he was successful in having most of the material returned within 48 hours. Karalivanos reported that children of the village had eaten a number of the quarter-pound blocks of plastic explosives under the impression that they were candy bars. The possible results of this gustatory experimentation worried the liaison officers, but they finally came to the conclusion that the explosive would probably only make the children ill -- not kill them. "Serve the little bastards right," was Karalivanos' comment.

The radio for Team No. 1 had been attached to Myers' parachute and dropped with him. While other members of the team had been occupied with regaining the stolen supplies, the radio technician had set up his equipment and attempted to get in touch with Cairo. Unable to make contact, it was discovered that the batteries were too weak. A subsequent questioning of the communications sergeant developed the interesting information that none of the technicians had been afforded an opportunity to inspect their equipment prior to landing.

After spending approximately a day in the immediate vicinity of their drop location, Team No. 1 received discouraging news from a local villager. Kaloskopi, the town nearest to the originally designated drop zone, had been raided by the Italians a few nights previously and a number of men, including Seferiades, had been taken prisoner. This was an indication that the Italians might have been informed of the drop and might even be aware of their plans. In addition, the village president of Karoutes was sure that the nearby Italian garrison was aware that an air drop had been made in that vicinity. Under the circumstances, it was considered advisable to move from the area. Since they were some distance south of the three viaducts, they arranged with Karalivanos for a guide to take them north. Meanwhile, having realized that they were many miles from Zervas' territory, Team No. 2 had also decided to move north.

En route, the two teams were reunited and eventually found a cave in which they holed up for several days while awaiting a previously arranged supply drop, scheduled for 9 October. During the course of their travels, the teams picked up several recruits: two Cypriots and two Palestinian Arabs, members of the British Expeditionary Force who had escaped from the Germans. They also acquired, as a guide, a part-time guerrilla who agreed to join the liaison officers.

The BLO's were disappointed not to have encountered any sizable guerrilla bands operating in the areas through which they passed. In fact, the villagers whom they questioned had never heard of Zervas and were extremely vague about Aris. The only guerrilla leader they had met was Karalivanos, whom they had understood was an important leader, but who had proved to have only four followers -- one of whom wanted to quit.

The 9 October supply drop was successfully accomplished, but on the following day the BLO's learned that the Italians had heard the plane and were searching for parachutists. Warning the villagers in the area to tell the Italians that only supplies had been dropped and that no parachutists were in the area, the two teams again moved to the north. Eventually they established semi-permanent headquarters in a cave near the village of Stromni, within striking distance of the three viaducts.

At every stop the two radio technicians had made valiant efforts to establish communications with Cairo. Their efforts, unfortunately, were unproductive as the batteries of the second set were also defective and the charging machine was broken. Unable to contact SOE Cairo, a messenger was sent to Athens to determine if Prometheus had received further instructions or information.

## Preparations for the Viaduct Operations

Before the sabotage operation could even be planned, it was necessary to determine which of the three viaducts would be the target and to make a careful survey of the surrounding area. On 25 October, Colonel Myers, accompanied by Captain Hamson and a local guide, set out on a reconnaissance.

From residents of villages near the railroad they obtained information on the frequency of trains and estimates of the strength of the viaduct guard details. Gorgopotamos, the most northerly of the three structures was guarded by about 80 men; Asopos had approximately 40 guards; and Papadia, the farthest south, was heavily guarded by more than 300 troops. All guard details were Italian, although there was a special patrol train, manned by Germans, which would respond to an emergency call. The two-car patrol train was kept on a siding at Lamia, just a few miles north of the Gorgopotamos viaduct, hitched to an engine with steam up and ready for instant dispatch.

Going first to the Papadia viaduct, the two BLO's were disappointed to find it surrounded by gently rolling hills with few trees, terrain offering little concealment for attackers. In addition, the estimate of 300 guards appeared to be accurate -- an attack operation would require a force of several hundred men. The reconnaissance group decided to check the other viaducts. Myers and Hamson were advised by their guide that Asopos would be extremely difficult to approach -- even for their small group -- and a check of the mouth of the Asopos ravine with its steep sides rising from a narrow, turbulent stream bed seemed to confirm his statement. Deciding to bypass Asopos, they pressed on toward Gorgopotamos. An examination of the structure, position, and environs of that viaduct convinced the British officers that it was a much more practical target than either of the others. Easier to approach than Asopos and, not only less heavily guarded than Papadia, it was more vulnerable to attack because there were covered routes of approach.

The Gorogopotamos viaduct was supported by seven piers, five of masonry and two of steel, between each of which ran 100-foot steel spans. The two steel piers, of which the tallest was about 70 feet in height, supported the southern end of the viaduct. If the tallest steel pier, which was second from the end, could be destroyed it would drop the two 100-foot spans into the ravine. After spending the better part of a day in examining the construction of the bridge through their field glasses, Myers and his party returned to their base camp near Stromni.

On 2 November, a few days after the completion of the reconnaissance, the messenger returned from Prometheus with definite information on the location of Zervas. Knowing that a considerable force of guerrillas would be necessary to accomplish the mission and believing that

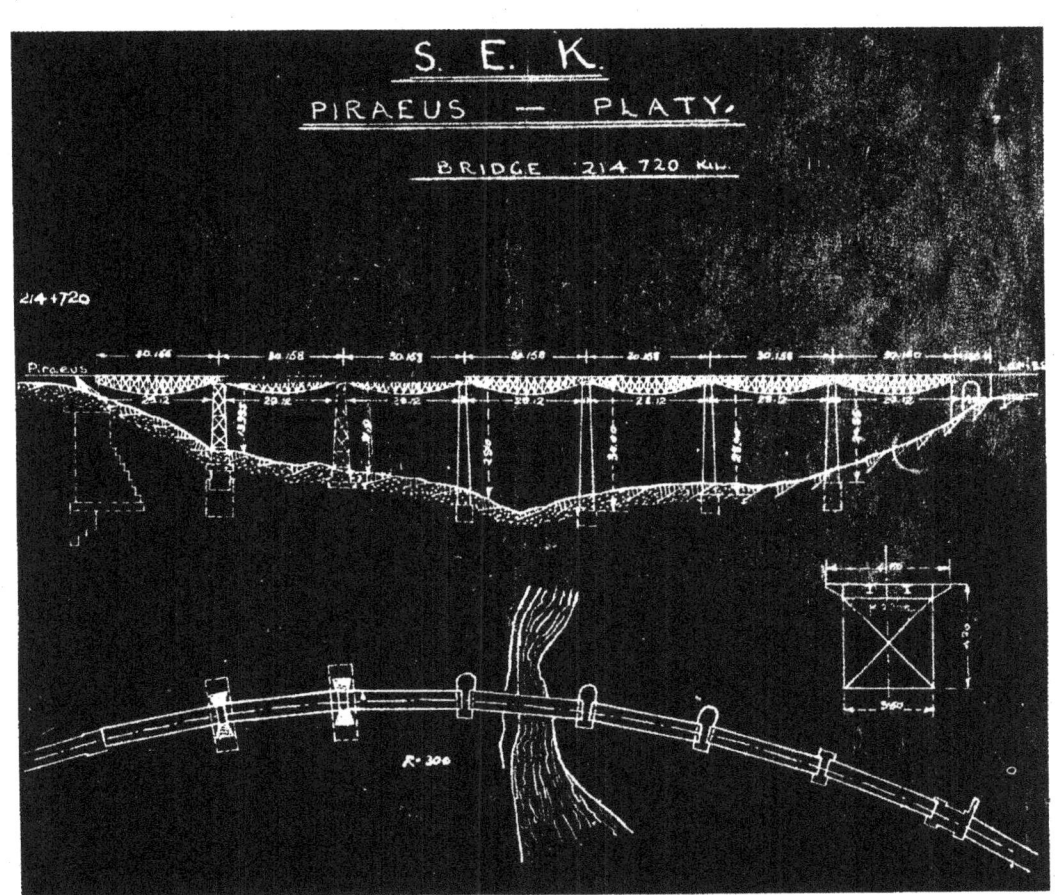

Side Elevation of GORGOTPOTAMOS Viaduct
(Reproduction of a blueprint used
in planning the sabotage operation)

Courtesy of the War History Branch,
Department of Internal Affairs,
New Zealand Government.

Zervas represented the only hope for such support, Woodhouse immediately set out for western Greece in an effort to find the guerrilla leader and solicit his aid.

Myers and Hamson having formed the opinion that the girders of the steel piers of Gorgopotamos were angle beams, the demolitions men set to work preparing appropriately shaped charges. The quarter-pound blocks of plastic explosive had hardened in the cold weather and had to be warmed before they could be molded into the larger charges which would be required to cut the massive steel girders. Obtaining boards from a local sawmill, the explosives were packed in forms that could be easily attached to the pier legs. Using parachute cord, the explosive charges were combined into easily carried one-man packs.

The BLO's soon began experiencing severe headaches which they attributed to the constant handling of explosives. They again wondered what the effect had been on the children who had eaten the quarter-pound blocks stolen from the first drop.

The BLO's found the period of waiting very depressing and their uncomfortable living conditions lowered morale still further. Already discouraged by their failure to contact any group of andartes large enough to carry out the mission, they were additionally disheartened to learn that the Italians had found and destroyed their principal cache of explosives, leaving them barely enough to do the job at Gorgopotamos. Although the radio operators had succeeded in making some progress with the radio, had faintly heard Cairo broadcasts, and had attempted a reply, they were still not in communication with their headquarters. Added to these discouragements were a number of personal difficulties. Unable to signal their locations or needs to Cairo, there had been no further supply drops. Their own food stores were exhausted and what little they obtained from the villagers of Stromni was of the poorest quality -- mostly beans and coarse corn bread. Both the beans and the bread disagreed with the Britishers and all of them suffered from diarrhoea -- an unhappy affliction that emphasized another problem -- they had no toilet paper. In fact, they had no paper of any kind and no deciduous trees or grass grew in the vicinity. The subsequent discovery that they were all infested with lice did nothing to improve their outlook on life. Hungry, uncomfortable, and generally unhappy, it is small wonder that the BLO's became edgy -- pressures built up, there were frequent flare-ups of temper and an increasing tendency to find fault with conditions and each other.

Further adding to their problems, the group learned that Karalivanos and his three followers had been ranging the countryside, seizing food from villagers in the name of the British liaison group. He had also attacked members of the Greek gendarmerie, an act which might well result in bringing Italian patrols into the Stromni area. Colonel Myers ordered Karalivanos to desist from his activities and, bluffing admirably, threatened him with arrest and shooting by the guerrillas that he hoped Woodhouse was bringing to Stromni. The bluff was successful and Karalivanos agreed to be more circumspect.

About the middle of November, Team No. 3 joined Colonel Myers' group, reporting that they had been dropped near Karpenision on 30 October. Why the drop had been made there was a mystery to everyone; it was some twenty-five miles -- more than two days' walk -- from the rail line and in an area heavily patrolled by the Italian garrison at Karpenision. The descent of the team had been greeted by rifle and mortar fire and the parachutists had become widely separated, only avoiding capture with some difficulty. Luckily none were injured in the landing or subsequent pursuit by Italian troops.

Team No. 3 had been helped in their escape by guerrillas under Aris who had sent them to join Colonel Myers, accompanied by a 25-man escort. The team brought no supplies or equipment, not having been able to recover any of the canisters that had been dropped with them. In addition, a knapsack containing maps and diagrams of the three viaducts had been lost and must be presumed to have fallen into the hands of the enemy, possibly compromising the entire operation. Colonel Myers was not happy with the performance of Major Cook's group, although the reinforcing of his small band by an additional four men was most welcome.

## Destruction of Gorgopotamos Viaduct

On 18 November, Woodhouse returned to the Stromni base camp, reporting that he had found Zervas and that the guerrilla leader was following a day behind with some fifty of his andartes. Aris was also moving into the Stromni area with a force of about one hundred.[17]

With a small army of 150 at hand, the explosive charges prepared, and the demolitions teams trained to do their job even while blindfolded, morale soared and the BLO's were anxious to get the operation under way. On meeting the two guerrilla leaders, Colonel Myers was rather surprised to find himself outranked by Zervas, who had recently promoted himself to the rank of general.[18] Aris was simply "Aris" -- he claimed no rank although it was obvious that he was regarded as a man of some consequence by his followers.

In consideration of his rank, Myers offered Zervas command of the operation; but the EDES leader turned it down in order not to antagonize Aris, who had the larger force and in whose territory they were operating. The final determination was that the destruction of the viaduct would be conducted under the joint command of Myers, Aris, and Zervas. Myers briefed his co-leaders on the operation and outlined his basic plan for its implementation. Zervas immediately dispatched four of his officers to make a reconnaissance of the terrain in the vicinity of Gorgopotamos and upon receiving their report a few days later, he expressed himself as being well satisfied with Myers' plan.

Due to animosity between Aris and Zervas, some command difficulties developed but the British officers were successful in smoothing over the differences and gaining the guerrilla leaders' joint agreement for the accomplishment of the project. Another hitch was threatened when Aris announced that he had been in touch with the EAM resistance organization in Lamia and reported that they were much opposed to the operation on the grounds that it was a highly impractical venture. Only after being assured that the destruction of the viaduct would be attempted, with or without his assistance, did Aris finally agree to co-operate.

The Gorgopotamos attack plan called for the formation of seven task forces. One group of twenty men would cut the only highway between the viaduct and Lamia to ambush any enemy reinforcements which might approach by that route. A second group of twenty, with one British officer, would place demolition charges on the tracks about two hundred yards north of the bridge. A group of approximately the same size, accompanied by two liaison officers, would place demolition charges on the rails about a mile south of the viaduct. Charges would not be detonated until after the viaduct had been destroyed, unless a train should approach. In that event, the charges would be blown in an attempt to derail the train and ambush its passengers. To prevent guards in other locations from being alerted, all three parties were to cut telephone and telegraph wires as soon as the attack commenced.

The fourth and fifth groups, each with a strength of thirty men would attack the Italian guard detachments at the viaduct -- one group at the north end and the other at the south. No liaison officers were to accompany either of these groups as the guerrillas insisted that their own leaders did not require outside assistance.

A sixth group had the highly important job of actually destroying the viaduct. The demolitions party was composed of four liaison officers, three of the escaped British prisoners, and six guerrillas.

The seventh group consisted of the headquarters and reserve. From a central location Myers, Woodhouse, Aris, and Zervas would control the operation. A small group of Zervas' guerrillas, led by his second in command, would be held in readiness to reinforce the attack teams.

The timing of each phase of the operation was of vital importance. Zero hour, the time of the attack, was set for 11 p.m. and the times required for each of the task forces to reach their destinations were carefully calculated.

On the morning of 24 November, the entire party set out for the Gorgopotamos viaduct, reaching a valley on the slopes of Mount Oiti during the late afternoon. There, in a deserted sawmill, the BLO's and the attack force made camp for the night.

It was cold and a heavy snow was falling. To keep themselves warm and dry, the ill-clad and often barefoot guerrillas built large fires. Since the encampment was in a deep depression and some distance from the viaduct they had no fear of ground observation and the heavy snow precluded any possibility of aerial observation. Even when a huge stack of lumber caught fire the BLO's were not unduly disturbed by the carelessness of the guerrillas.

Moving on the next day, the little army assumed its task force formations, each heading toward its objective. By midafternoon, the headquarters unit, the two principal attack forces, and the demolitions team had reached the edge of a forest on the north slope of Mount Oiti. Concealed by the trees they laid over awaiting nightfall and the time to advance to their final positions. Shortly after dusk the groups began advancing to their attack positions.

A system of signals had been agreed upon for control of the action: when the group attacking the northern end of the viaduct had driven off the guards, a white Very flare would be fired; the group attacking the south end would fire a similar signal, using a red flare, when their objective had been attained. Since the demolitions party would be working under the south end of the bridge, upon seeing the red flare they would move in to place their charges. When the charges were in place, and before lighting the fuses, the team would blow three blasts on a whistle. Three minute fuses would give all men an opportunity to take cover. When the operation was concluded or in the event it had to be aborted, the signal for recall would be a green flare fired by the headquarters group.

By the designated hour, all groups were in position and the simultaneous attack on the two guard detachments started only a few minutes late. The attack on the south end went well, but the group at the north end ran into heavy fire which caused the inexperienced andartes to fall back. The reserves, commanded by Kominos Pyromaglou, Zervas' deputy, were thrown in to bolster the northern attack. Even this additional strength made no immediate change in the battle situation and, with no progress apparent, Zervas became discouraged and announced that he would fire the green flare -- call off the entire operation. This action might well have been disastrous since Aris had already gone on record as saying that if the attempt failed that night, his men could never be induced to try it again.

Fortunately for the eventual success of the operation, the signal pistol could not be found -- Pyromaglou had taken it with him. Woodhouse went forward to find Zervas' deputy and retrieve the pistol and soon returned with word that things were going better at the north end; Pyromaglou expected to have the Italians routed very soon.

After about an hour of fighting, the red flare was fired from the south end. The demolitions team rushed in to place their charges. Making their way to the tallest steel pier, they were disconcerted -- in fact, horrified -- to find that the shape of the steel supports had been wrongly diagnosed. Instead of being the right-angle girders for which the charges had been so carefully prepared, the supports were U-shaped and the charges would not fit. It was necessary for the four liaison officers to take them all apart and reform them. The work of reforming the charges was aided by the bright moonlight, but the brightness of the night also helped the Italians to zero-in on the group with a light mortar. Fortunately, although several shells landed in the immediate vicinity, no one was hit nor were the explosives detonated.

With the additional work, the placing of the charges consumed nearly an hour and meanwhile the battle for the north end of the viaduct still raged. It finally required the presence of Colonel Myers to inspire the <u>andartes</u> to close in and wipe out the last of the resistance at that end of the bridge. Eventually, the white flare was fired and almost immediately the blast of the demolitions team's warning whistle was heard.

Three minutes later, the charges detonated and the big steel pier, with an eight-foot section blown out of each leg, settled in a twisted mass. The two spans on either side of the pier dropped into the ravine. Returning immediately, the demolitions team placed additional charges to complete the wreckage and insure that repair would be even more difficult. While the second series of charges was being laid, an explosion and firing from the north gave warning that reinforcements from Lamia were en route by rail. Placing the new charges required several minutes and sounds of firing from the north grew steadily closer. Myers and Woodhouse worked their way as close as possible to the demolitions team and, shouting across the gorge, urged them to hurry. At last the charges were emplaced, 90-second fuses were ignited, and the team ran for the safety of a nearby culvert. Simultaneously with the detonation of the explosives, the green Very signal was fired and a general withdrawal began.

Early on the 26th, most of the force gathered once more at the rendezvous in the forest on Mount Oiti. The only task force unit not yet accounted for was the southern ambush group which had a much greater distance to cover. Leaving a liaison group behind to pick up stragglers, the force moved on again to the sawmill where they had spent the night of the 24th.

The group which had guarded the northern approach to the viaduct reported that they had blown the track at the approach of what proved to be a special patrol train but had failed to derail it. The train had been stopped, however, and the guerrillas had inflicted heavy casualties on the reinforcing detachment. The task force had fallen back slowly and when the green signal was seen had disengaged and withdrawn. Later, the southern task force reported that they had been undisturbed throughout the entire operation and upon seeing the withdrawal signal had blown a section of the track and withdrawn without difficulty.

Damage to the viaduct had been substantial and it was estimated that it would require at least two months to effect repairs.[19] The operation had been a complete success -- only two or three andartes wounded, none seriously -- although the BLO's saddened the news that in reprisal the Italians had shot fourteen men from Lamia. Included among the victims was one Costa Pistoli who had been extremely helpful to Myers and Hamson during their reconnaissance. The andartes, in turn, had one of their youngest recruits win his spurs by decapitating the one Italian prisoner that had been taken.

After Gorgopotamos

Withdrawing to the southeast as individuals or in small groups, the entire attack force reassembled at Mavrolitharion. Here, where they had started for Gorgopotamos two days before, the BLO's and guerrillas were able to get their first real rest since the start of the operation.

Since radio communication with Cairo had not yet been effected, Myers sent a runner to Prometheus, in Athens, with a message for SOE Cairo. In it he reported the success of their mission and suggested a place and time for the evacuation of his group; asking that the submarine pick them up on the west coast, at the mouth of the Akheron River, between 22 and 25 December.

After a brief rest, Zervas announced that affairs in Epirus required his attention and that he must return to his home territory without delay. The British were to accompany him and then push on to the coast and their rendezvous with the submarine. Aris also announced that he would move southwest into Roumeli to take care of important business in that region.

Prior to their departure, Myers and Woodhouse made a determined effort to bring Aris and Zervas together, hoping to achieve a unification of the Greek guerrilla movement. Although an informal agreement to respect each other's territory was made, Aris refused to consider unification at that time. He did, however, leave the door open for future negotiations. He asked that a liaison officer be assigned to his headquarters and was told by Woodhouse that every effort would be made to send him a representative as soon as possible.

Colonel Myers made a speech to the two guerrilla forces in which he thanked the two leaders for their great assistance and congratulated them on the achievement of such an important mission. In conclusion, he told that he was recommending Aris, Zervas and several others for decorations. Aris, with characteristic bluntness, replied that he wasn't interested in a decoration: "I would much rather have shoes for my andartes." Myers promised to do what he could about supplies for ELAS and, after making Aris a gift of 250 gold sovereigns, the British group started west with Zervas.

Although much of their trip was through ELAS territory, the first part assumed the character of a triumphal march. At every village and hamlet through which they passed, the populace turned out to cheer and listen to a speech by Zervas. Farther west, Italian patrols were out in considerable strength and the entire force was required to hole up in a mountain village for two days. Subsequently, enemy patrol activity made it necessary to take several long and difficult detours over the most rugged of mountain paths. On 8 December, the entire group, including a sizable band of EDES <u>andartes</u> which had been picked up at Viniani, arrived at Zervas' headquarters in Megalokhari.

Estimating that the trip to the rendezvous point would consume another twelve days, the BLO's had to press on after only one day's rest. As guides and escort, Zervas assigned a small detachment under the command of Captain Mihalis, his adjutant. Since no confirmation of the message requesting the submarine pick-up had been received, there were some misgivings among the British as to the advisability of starting the long and hazardous journey. Myers, however, was confident that his suggestion would be followed by SOE Cairo and it was decided that, as a calculated risk, the trip would be worth the effort. With their guide and escort detachment furnished by Zervas and the four Cypriot and Palestinian recruits, the BLO's set out on 10 December, leaving Woodhouse and Marinos with two radio operators at the EDES headquarters.

In spite of the agreement that ELAS and EDES would respect each other's territory, Myers and his party had scarcely started for the rendezvous point when Aris, with about 400 men, moved across the Achelous River and entered Zervas' operational zone. Woodhouse met with the ELAS leader and strongly suggested that he withdraw. Aris replied that there had been an air drop in the area and that he had come to claim his share. It was explained that the contents of the drop had already been distributed to EDES and that ELAS would receive drops later. Still unconvinced, Aris continued his advance and EDES forces fell back. Finally, Woodhouse was successful in bringing Zervas and Aris together and, after mutually disagreeing on a number of subjects, the two guerrilla leaders came to the conclusion that no useful purpose could be served by fighting each other. Aris left the Epirus area to return to Roumeli.

Meanwhile, the British group heading for the mouth of the Akheron was pushing on in expectation of being evacuated to Egypt. Since their route would take them through a region in which there were no <u>andarte</u> bands to provide protection, it was considered advisable to travel at night. The presence of numerous Italian patrols required the taking of long and arduous detours and this, combined with the necessity to travel under cover of darkness, slowed their progress. As they made their way westward, the country through which they passed grew poorer and poorer. Although the Greek peasants shared what little food they had, the little became progressively less and the entire party soon began to suffer badly from hunger and fatigue.

Eventually reaching their evacuation point, the twelve Britishers spent three miserable nights, including Christmas Eve, hopefully flashing a signal light out to sea. On Christmas Day a runner arrived with a message from Woodhouse that no submarine would be coming. The message included the information that new orders for the group were en route, being hand-carried by an officer who was expected to be dropped to Megalokhari within a day or two. The implication of this -- that they would be required to remain in Greece indefinitely -- was most disheartening.

The trip from the rendezvous point back to Zervas' headquarters was a nightmare. Already seriously weakened by lack of food, suffering from loss of sleep, and physically exhausted, the condition of all degenerated seriously. Morale, which was already low, sank completely out of sight. To make matters worse, it was necessary to return by a more circuitous route and to make a number of difficult detours to avoid the many Italian patrols which were searching for them. Finally, during the first week of January 1943, they reached Megalokhari to find that, during their absence, the Italians had attacked the village and burned most of it.

Zervas was off to the south harassing the Italians and Woodhouse was with him. Marinos was, however, waiting for them and the totally exhausted men were able to get their first real meal and rest in many days. Colonel Myers received his new orders and was gratified to learn that communications with Cairo had been firmly established.

# CHAPTER III

## NEW MISSIONS AND ATTEMPTS AT UNFICATION[1]
(1943)

### The British Military Mission Remains

The December 1942 directive from SOE Cairo reconstituted the British Military Mission on a permanent basis with Colonel Myers in command. As an old soldier he was philosophical about this change in his personal situation, but he was distressed that no provision had been made for the evacuation of the other members of the group. With the exception of those assigned to Zervas' headquarters, the entire group of BLO's had volunteered with the understanding that they would be returned to Egypt after the conclusion of the viaduct operation. Upon being queried as to their desires, after the receipt of the new orders, all but two of them requested evacuation from Greece as soon as possible.

Moving to Skoulikaria, Zervas' new headquarters, Myers learned of the ELAS incursion into EDES territory and directed Captain Nat Barker, one of those who had agreed to remain, to join Aris as liaison officer. Myers also requested Cairo to set up a new evacuation plan and, pending a reply, did not assign specific duties to the other BLO's.

With radio communication well established with SOE Cairo, messages came in almost daily. One of these advised the BMM that a group of six highly-regarded Greek Army colonels had banded together in Athens with the object of unifying the resistance and guerrilla movements in all of Greece. It was believed by SOE and members of the Greek Government-in-Exile that this group might be the means of effecting a coalition of all the disparate interests involved in the resistance and guerrilla movements. It was suggested that Woodhouse be stationed in Athens to act as liaison officer between the colonels and the BMM. Although Zervas and the BLO's were convinced that guerrilla operations could only be controlled from the field, it was agreed that Woodhouse would visit Athens and confer with the six colonels.

His knowledge of the Greeks -- their language, customs, and politics -- made Woodhouse an excellent choice for the conduct of discussions. Unfortunately, his appearance made him a poor selection as far as avoiding detection was concerned. Woodhouse, six feet tall and red-haired, would stand out among the short, swarthy Greeks like the proverbial sore thumb. As it later developed, Woodhouse did have a very narrow escape. A raid by occupation security forces picked up Prometheus, with whom Woodhouse was in close contact, and the British officer only avoided capture when the EAM underground organization spirited him out of Athens.

Shortly after the departure of Woodhouse for Athens, an Italian raid on Skoulikaria forced the BMM headquarters to move to Avlaki, a short distance to the southeast. The flight of the BLO's was complicated by the fact that Colonel Myers was virtually in a coma -- critically ill with pneumonia. The BLO's stayed in Avlaki for several weeks while their commander recovered and was once more capable of making plans to implement the orders which were coming in regularly from Cairo. Unwilling to be idle when there was so much to be done, the BLO's awaiting evacuation agreed to continue working on BMM projects until arrangements could be made to get them back to Cairo.

Although SOE Cairo did not schedule any major sabotage operations for the immediate future, the andarte bands were to be assisted and encouraged to harass the enemy forces and to disrupt their lines of communication. The principal tasks of the BMM would be to organize the guerrilla movement as much as possible, request and receive air drops, and supervise the distribution of arms, ammunition, and other supplies which would be dropped.

The fact that there were no large-scale operations does not mean that there was a cessation of guerrilla activity. Andarte bands all over Greece executed ambushes, mined bridges and highways, cut railroads, and destroyed telephone and telegraph lines. One popular andarte tactic was to cut a wire line and mine the poles adjacent to the break so that enemy soldiers who attempted to repair the lines were blown up. A variation of this tactic was to station a sharpshooter in the hills above the wire break and shoot the repairmen off the tops of the poles.[2]

On the east-west highway from Ioannina to Trikkala and Larisa, ELAS bands continually harassed convoys and patrols. Man-made landslides, roadblocks, and ambushes were combined to deny the enemy the use of any portion of this only cross-country highway in central Greece. The five thousand-foot-high Metsovon Pass which controlled access to Ioannina from the north as well as the east was blocked throughout most of 1943. On all four main highways approaching Larisa, there were so many ambushes that the Italians found it necessary, on several occasions, to supply their garrison by air. In western Thessaly and Epirus,

Zervas continued his early tactics of destroying Italian convoys and erecting roadblocks on the Ioannina-Arta highway. His force was also active in ambushing patrols. In many areas the Italians were compelled to evacuate small towns and villages and were completely bottled up in towns where they could maintain large garrisons.

In addition to ambushes, destruction of bridges, and the blocking of roads by creating landslides, the guerrillas employed other and more ingenious methods of impeding traffic. Four-pronged metal forms, whose tetrahedroid shape caused them always to fall with a point up, were scattered over the most frequently used highways.[3] The constant stopping to repair punctures not only delayed convoys but also exposed personnel to snipers or guerrilla band attacks. Later, the guerrillas received from the British large numbers of small, concrete-covered mines which detonated when run over by a vehicle. Strewn along the roads, they were almost impossible to distinguish from the natural rocks and their concrete construction made them difficult to detect with conventional mine detectors.[4]

Seeking to channel guerrilla activities into co-ordinated operations which would directly benefit the Middle East Command, in early February the BMM requested guidance on target priorities. SOE Cairo replied that the _andartes_ should be encouraged to sabotage oil storage and transport facilities as well as mines and mineral transport, with particular emphasis on chromium. The BLO's were also requested to promote industrial sabotage "without bangs": slow-downs, strikes, and manufacture of faulty parts. This second request was not, of course, directly connected with guerrilla operations but was in the province of the resistance movements' underground organizations of the cities. The suggested guerrilla priorities were immediately forwarded to Barker for relay to Aris, along with information that the number of supply drops would be stepped up during the next month. Barker reported within a few days that Aris and his bands were co-operating and attacking the targets indicated.

## Efforts to Achieve Unification

On 4 February 1943, Colonel Stefanos Sarafis visited the chief of the BMM, asking for support of guerrilla bands he was in the process of forming under the aegis of the AAA resistance organization. In a joint conference with General Zervas it was suggested that all guerrilla bands be united under the name of National Bands of Greece. Although it was recognized that EAM/ELAS would undoubtedly refuse to cooperate, it was believed that if that organization could be presented with a _fait accompli_ -- a strong centralized union of all other bands -- it would be forced to join.

In dealing with the various resistance and guerrilla organizations the BLO's had found themselves increasingly involved in the complexities of Greek politics, a thing they were anxious to avoid. Hoping that the guerrillas could be encouraged to get on with the war and let political problems wait until the Axis had been defeated, the BMM strongly advocated that the National Bands be completely nonpolitical. Both Zervas and Sarafis were in full agreement with the suggestion.

Colonel Myers and the other members of the BMM were enthusiastic about the National Bands concept and a message sent to SOE Cairo informing that headquarters of the contemplated action received a prompt reply approving and endorsing the move. Only one change was made in the plan as presented: it had been suggested that General Plastiras, then in southern France, be brought back to Greece to head up the National Bands; reluctant to further complicate an already complicated political situation, SOE Cairo did not approve this suggestion and recommended that the new organization operate directly under the Commander-in-Chief, Middle East.

Shortly thereafter, the National Bands' cause was strengthened when Colonel Psaros, who was building a guerrilla force under the sponsorship of EKKA, agreed to support the move.

The possibility that the six colonels in Athens might direct the new movement was rather definitely eliminated when Woodhouse returned from his visit to Athens on 20 February. He reported that he had been unable to see all six of the colonels but that those he had seen had not impressed him with their practicality. They were visionaries and completely uninformed about the guerrillas and the areas in which they were operating. Their goal seemed to be the formation of a secret army which would rise as the day of liberation approached -- to drive the Axis forces from Greece and, as a revitalized Greek Army, go on to help the Allies win final victory. It was their theory that all _andarte_ bands would be absorbed into the new army. Woodhouse was of the opinion that, while the six colonels might be of some service after liberation, they would be of no use in effecting the unification of the resistance and guerrilla movements.

The great weakness of the National Bands scheme was the fact that only Zervas' EDES force was strong enough to stand against the fast-growing EAM/ELAS forces. Unfortunately, his location in the western Pindus Mountains, with strong ELAS bands between his territory and eastern Greece, would prevent his providing protection to the other members of the National Bands. If ELAS chose to oppose the coalition forcibly, the small independent bands would be too weak to stand against the now considerable strength of the Communist-controlled organization.

Apparently thinking that its approval of the National Bands concept was all that was required to effect unification, SOE Cairo almost immediately set up a most ambitious program for the BMM and the Greek guerrillas. A new directive called for the conduct of guerrilla operations throughout all of Greece, with particular emphasis on the Attica, southern Pindus Mountains, and Peloponnesus areas. It was also requested that liaison with the resistance forces in Albania and southern Jugoslavia be established. The over-all plan called for preparations being made for greatly accelerated activity in the summer -- to be co-ordinated with Allied landings in Sicily and a simultaneous invasion of the Dodecannese Islands.

To organize the andartes for this accelerated program, the BMM divided Greece into five operational areas. The BMM would assign teams consisting of a senior BLO and several assistants to Epirus, Roumeli, Macedonia, and the area around Mount Olympus. Each would be responsible for the organization of his district and, although he would have direct radio contact with Cairo, he would be under the operational control of the BMM headquarters. Because of the distance involved and difficulties of communication, the BMM recommended that the Peloponnesus be eliminated from its zone of responsibility. It was suggested that a separate command be established there under direct control of SOE Cairo. In forwarding his plan to Cairo, Colonel Myers advised that the newly assigned missions would require a number of additional liaison officers, radio technicians, and radios.

On 4 March, Colonel Myers learned that Sarafis had been captured by an ELAS band, led by one Kozakas, and charged with collaborating. At the same time, Captain Hamson reported that another ELAS band had attacked and dispersed a small band to which he had been assigned as liaison officer. Vlakhos, leader of the independent band, had fled and was in hiding, in fear of his life. The BMM chief, angered by the treachery of ELAS, seriously contemplated breaking off all relations with that organization. Zervas wanted to attack Kozakas and his belligerent mood was not mollified by the receipt of a threatening letter from the ELAS leader demanding that Vlakhos be turned over to him.

A full report, including Myers' intention of taking drastic action, was immediately sent off to Cairo. In reply, Cairo emphasized that on no account should relations with EAM/ELAS be disrupted and quoted reports from the BLO in the Mount Olympus area that indicated that Sarafis was a collaborator.[5]

## ELAS and the National Bands Agreement

Deciding to delay no longer in attempting to secure the support of EAM/ELAS for the National Bands concept, Myers and Woodhouse prepared a 12-point document outlining the terms of its organization.

Taking several copies of the agreement with him, Colonel Myers set out to find Kozakas, Aris, or other representatives of EAM/ELAS whom he hoped to win over to some sort of unification agreement and, incidentally, effect the release of Sarafis.

Arriving at the village of Kolokythia, toward the end of March, Myers met Aris and an EAM representative who went under the name of Evmaios, but whose real name was Andreas Tzimas.[6] Myers denounced Kozakas' actions and threatened to cut off all military aid to ELAS if Sarafis was not freed and an end put to such high-handed procedures. Tzimas explained that the whole thing had been a misunderstanding and that Sarafis and his chief assistant were now free. On meeting with Sarafis, the BMM chief was amazed to find that instead of being angered at his captors, he had executed a complete about face and had become an EAM/ELAS convert. When queried by Colonel Myers, Sarafis staunchly defended his conversion:

> In answer, I told Colonel Eddie /Myers/ that during the three months I had been in the mountains what I had seen had convinced me that, in order to secure for the Greek people concord and a smooth transition to liberation and civilian life, and in order to avoid all clashes and later a civil war, the best solution was that there should be one organization and one guerrilla army and not various chieftains. As such a basic organization I suggested EAM, which was nation-wide and well organized.[7]

Later, of course, it developed that Sarafis had not only espoused the EAM/ELAS cause, but had accepted the position of military commander of all ELAS forces. His antagonism toward the British became very marked and from that time on, the BMM received a minimum of co-operation from "General" Sarafis.

During the course of the meetings with Aris and Tzimas the National Bands plan of unification was discussed and a copy of the proposed agreement was given to Tzimas who agreed to present it to the EAM Central Committee in Athens.

The National Bands Agreement, as prepared by Myers and Woodhouse, did not attempt to bring all bands under the leadership of one man or one resistance organization. Rather, it called for the formation of a loose confederation under which Greece would be divided into districts, each under a military commander. All men would be free to join any guerrilla band they wished and all resistance and guerrilla organizations would be free to raise and maintain bands in any part of the country, provided they co-operated with the district military commander. Although, in general, bands would operate only in the area of their origin, by co-ordination through the district commander bands of one area would be encouraged to lend assistance to bands in other areas for military as well as logistic support. Arbiters of all differences between district commanders or bands would be the BMM or the senior BLO of each district.[8]

During the period following Colonel Myers' meeting with Aris and Tzimas, the situation in the mountains of Greece seemed to be improving. Radio communication between the BMM and Cairo was working well, additional liaison officers were being dropped in, supply drops had been stepped up, and there appeared to be some hope that EAM/ELAS might subscribe to the National Bands Agreement. In addition, the BMM received word that ELAS units had, in accordance with British desires, made several successful raids on chromium mines -- one at Dhomokos, in southern Thessaly, having been put out of operation for several weeks.

The Gorgopotamos viaduct had been repaired and, with the exception of delays caused by minor acts of sabotage, the Salonika-Athens rail line was back to almost normal operation. For some time, the BMM had been considering the destruction of another major rail facility, preferably the Asopos viaduct which was situated just south of Gorgopotamos. Early in 1943 a BLO group had been assigned to the project and, in conjunction with the senior BLO in the area, had been reconnoitering the area and studying possible methods of attack. The senior BLO had also made contact with Aris and had been promised full ELAS support for the operation.

On 12 May, Colonel Myers, who had arrived in the Roumeli district to check on the progress of the operation, was incensed to learn that ELAS had been attacking other guerrilla bands in the area. One EDES and an independent band had been dispersed and their leaders taken prisoner. In addition, Aris had just recently surrounded, disarmed, and scattered the EKKA force -- Colonel Psaros and several of his officers being held captive. Going at once to Stromni, Myers remonstrated with Aris who simply replied that he had received instructions from EAM that only ELAS bands were to be permitted in Roumeli. Myers demanded a conference with a responsible representative from the EAM Central Committee.

Traveling to Koukouvitsa (Kaloskopi) with Aris, the BMM chief met Tzimas and Sarafis on 16 May and for the next few weeks was engaged in a series of conferences with the ELAS leaders. At the outset, Myers was informed that a General Headquarters for ELAS had been established, under the joint command of Sarafis, as military commander; Tzimas, as political advisor; and Aris, as *capetan*. Hereafter, it was announced, no action would be taken by any ELAS band unless it was previously approved by GHQ, ELAS. This dictate applied to the Asopos operation which Tzimas claimed was far too hazardous an undertaking for ELAS forces. In spite of Aris' previous agreement to render full co-operation, the new headquarters refused to sanction ELAS' participation and suggested several alternatives -- each involving only minor sabotage. Myers' insistence that only the destruction of the Asopos viaduct would cause disruption of the Athens-Salonika rail line for an extended period, fell on deaf ears. The three ELAS leaders were then informed that the BMM would accomplish the task without guerrilla assistance.

Fast losing patience, Myers demanded an explanation for the imprisonment of the independent guerrilla leaders and the disarming of their forces. The ELAS leaders stoutly maintained that the captured EDES band had provoked the incident by attacking ELAS *andartes*. Aris added that all bands other than ELAS were collaborating and that only ELAS was fighting the fascist occupiers. Tzimas proved more conciliatory and explained that the disarming of Psaros' band had all been a mistake -- Aris had misunderstood his orders -- and not only agreed to free Psaros and the other leaders, but to restore seized arms and permit the reforming of their bands. General Sarafis, who held Colonel Psaros in high esteem, attempted to recruit him to EAM/ELAS, offering him command of all ELAS and EKKA forces in Roumeli.[9]

Somewhat mollified by the release of Psaros, the BMM commander brought up the subject of the National Bands Agreement and was told that EAM/ELAS was prepared to sign an amended version. Tzimas explained that the EAM Central Committee objected to the submitted agreement on the grounds that it placed the guerrilla bands completely under BMM control. The EAM amended agreement eliminated almost all mention of the BLO's as far as direction of the guerrilla effort was concerned. With the exception of the changes which radically reduced British influence, the amended version was much the same as the original and the BMM chief recalled that his BLO's always held one trump card -- they controlled the air drops.

While the BMM was willing to accept the EAM version -- out of sheer desperation and the pressing need to achieve some sort of a working agreement -- the Middle East Command refused to sanction it. The C-in-C, Middle East, definitely felt that he who pays the piper calls the tune. If the guerrilla bands of Greece were to be supplied by the Middle East Command they would work under its direction, and that direction would come through the senior British officer in Greece.

In a subsequent conference with Tzimas, Colonel Myers tried to persuade the EAM representative to accept changes in the National Bands Agreement which would make it acceptable to the Middle East Command. Tzimas refused to accept any compromise but made a surprising concession at the conclusion of the talks. He agreed that ELAS would abide by the provisions of the amended version just as if it had been signed by both parties.

## ELAS General Headquarters

The new ELAS general headquarters divided the country into major operational areas, each having its own headquarters or general command. As announced by GHQ, ELAS, the major commands and strengths were:

    Macedonia Headquarters . . . . . . . . . . 4,500 men
    Thessaly Headquarters . . . . . . . . . . 4,000 "
    Roumeli General Command . . . . . . . . 3,000 "
    Epirus General Command . . . . . . . . . . 500 "

Within each of the major command areas, subcommands were established, their number being determined by the size of the area and the strength of the guerrilla force. The Peloponnesus General Command and ELAS units in the vicinity of Athens were not under GHQ, ELAS but were controlled directly by the ELAS Central Command, an organization in Athens closely associated with the EAM Central Committee.

One of the first acts of the new general headquarters was to announce military commanders for the major area commands and to issue a series of directives for their guidance. Among the latter were instructions to the Roumeli General Command to send a force of sixty picked <u>andartes</u> to the Peloponnesus to reinforce and assist in the build-up of the comparatively small ELAS force operating in that area.

According to General Sarafis, the formation of the ELAS general headquarters did not meet with the whole-hearted approval of the BMM or Middle East Command. He records both as raising the objection that the creation of a general headquarters was premature and unnecessary at that time. ELAS countered with the contention that the British were motivated by self-interest and a desire to exercise absolute control over Greece and its people.

It is doubtful if the British would have objected to the formation of a central guerrilla command as being "premature," since the major effort of the BMM had been directed to effecting some degree of unification of the guerrilla movement. It is probable, however, that the British felt that the formation of the general headquarters by ELAS was premature in that it was announced while the BMM was attempting to establish a joint general headquarters for all guerrilla forces. ELAS' contention that the British wished to exercise control over Greece and its people is also open to question. That the BMM wished to direct and control the guerrilla movement is obvious. They felt that if Greek guerrilla operations were to support the over-all Allied strategy effectively, the Middle East Command should have direction and control of the guerrilla movement.

One of the operations suggested by GHQ, ELAS as a substitute for Asopos was the destruction of the railroad tunnel near Kournovon, northeast of Lamia. Colonel Myers objected to this on the basis that it was actually only minor sabotage. German earth-moving equipment would clear the tunnel in a few days, whereas the blowing of the viaduct would disrupt the railroad for several weeks, possibly months. It was finally agreed that the BMM would supply ELAS with explosives to accomplish the destruction of the tunnel as an independent objective. The operation was carried out on 1 June and General Sarafis reported its success to Colonel Myers:

The force carrying out the action had so timed it that a passing Italian train was trapped in part of the tunnel and destroyed with it. Besides the equipment wrecked, 500-600 Italians had been killed. Communications were cut for several days. I told Colonel Eddie [Myers] who was delighted and transmitted the information to Cairo at once. In reprisal, the Italians took 118 patriots from the Larissa concentration camp, nearly all members of EAM, and executed them on the site of the disaster.

In his account of the operation Colonel Myers does not mention being "delighted" and adds that at least forty Greek hostages, forced to ride in the first car of the train, were also killed. The BMM chief doubted if disrupting the railroad for a few days and the killing of five to six hundred enemy troops justified the sacrifice of so many Greek lives.[11] In the opinion of the British, the Asopos viaduct was still a much more worthwhile target.

In accordance with instructions, previously received from Cairo, the BMM chief asked ELAS to undertake an accelerated program of sabotage during the period of 21 June to 14 July. This campaign would parallel large-scale Allied operations -- possibly an invasion of Greece or some of the Aegean islands. ELAS was reluctant to participate on the grounds that the sabotage campaign would take a heavy toll of guerrilla lives and result in severe reprisals against the civilian populace. GHQ, ELAS agreed, however, to consider the matter and would make plans for the three-week campaign of intensified activity while a final decision was pending.

## Further Efforts at Unification

On 5 June, in another effort to bring EDES and ELAS together, the BMM arranged a meeting at Liaskovo (Petroton) between Zervas and the triumverate commanding ELAS. The conference got off to a bad start when the ELAS leaders objected to Zervas appearing in their territory with a bodyguard of 250 men. They claimed this was evidence of lack of faith and that the entry of so large a body of EDES andartes into ELAS territory without prior clearance contravened the spirit of the National Bands Agreement.

Acceptance of the National Bands Agreement did not appear to be imminent, however, and as an interim measure the BMM proposed the formation of a joint general headquarters. In addition to the chief of BMM, the joint headquarters would have a representative from EDES and ELAS -- preferably Zervas and Sarafis. While there was general agreement that such a headquarters would be advantageous, there was no agreement regarding its composition. Tzimas, Aris, and Sarafis insisted that ELAS should be represented by all three of its leaders, basing their contention on the fact that their tripartite command structure required decisions to be approved jointly. ELAS also insisted that an ELAS preponderance of headquarters representation was justified by its greater numerical strength. In proof, they submitted the following membership figures which were claimed to be accurate: ELAS, 12,500; EDES, 500; and EKKA, 200.[12] Since Zervas claimed some 7,000 members of EDES at that time, it would appear that the quoted figures may have been weighted somewhat in favor of ELAS.[13] There is, however, no doubt that ELAS did greatly outnumber all other Greek guerrilla organizations.

Zervas absolutely refused to agree to a joint command in which ELAS would always have a majority. After two days of fruitless argument, the BMM offered a compromise: Colonel Myers would establish a joint headquarters to which each guerrilla force would send a liaison officer who would be empowered to make decisions binding upon his organization. ELAS was only partially in agreement with this arrangement. While agreeing to send a liaison officer to the joint headquarters, it was made clear that he would be empowered only to accept and receive messages.

On 15 June, Brigadier Myers made an effort to determine whether or not ELAS was actually going to proceed with the intensified sabotage campaign scheduled to begin on the 21st.[14] Meeting Sarafis at Metsovon he asked for a definite commitment. During the course of their discussions, it was agreed that ELAS would be officially recognized as one of the field armies of the Middle East Command. A document defining this new position of ELAS was signed by both parties and the ELAS military commander announced his willingness to go ahead with the campaign of destruction. On his part, Myers assured Sarafis of increased drops of arms and demolitions in the immediate future.

In this discussion, as in most of their dealings with EAM/ELAS, the British were in a difficult position. Directives to the BMM from the Middle East Command required the full co-operation of all guerrilla forces for implementation, but the highly independent ELAS command did not co-operate with the willingness of EDES. Usually, agreements with ELAS were only achieved after a tight "horse-trading" session. The BMM needed ELAS and ELAS needed British arms, equipment, and gold. The BMM would approach ELAS with a request for co-operation, ELAS would be reluctant, the BMM would then threaten to cut off all support, simultaneously making a counteroffer to increase the number of supply drops if ELAS would co-operate. Somewhere along the barter line, a point of agreement would be reached.

The conference which resulted in securing ELAS co-operation in the diversionary sabotage campaign was a typical "horse trade." Sarafis claims that he demanded that ELAS be recognized as a field army under the C-in-C, Middle East and when this status was clearly defined he readily agreed to carry out the required sabotage operations.[15] Myers gives another version, saying that he coerced Sarafis into agreeing to act under the orders of the C-in-C, Middle East by threatening withdrawal of British logistic support and then offering ELAS the major portion of seventy air drops expected during July.

Shortly after ELAS was recognized as a component of the Middle East Command, Brigadier Myers was able to inform GHQ, ELAS that the BMM was now authorized to sign the amended version of the National Bands Agreement with a few minor changes. The ELAS command agreed that the changes were agreeable to them, but stated that such a long time had elapsed since the agreement was last discussed, it would be necessary to send the document to the EAM Central Committee for final approval. At last there seemed to be some progress toward unification, but that progress was distressingly slow.

As the date set for the start of the three-week campaign of accelerated sabotage had approached, the number of air drops had been greatly increased. Throughout May and early June large quantities of demolitions had been distributed to the guerrillas and were being held in readiness. Although ELAS constantly complained that supplies were inadequate and that EDES and EKKA were being favored over ELAS, Brigadier Myers avers that distribution was made fairly.

Although not considered as being a part of the long-planned sabotage campaign, the blowing of the Asopos viaduct served as a most impressive opening.

## Destruction of Asopos Viaduct

The Asopos viaduct crossed a precipitous gorge, through which the Asopos River raced, some 200 feet below the bridge. The southern half of the 200-yard-long viaduct was supported by a series of tall stone piers. At the north end a 100-yard span was supported by two steel arches cantilevered out from heavy stone piers on either side of the gorge. The structure was guarded by a detachment of only fifty men, but they were Germans who would be more alert and less subject to panic than the Italians encountered at Gorgopotamos.

Several plans for the destruction operation were made and discarded. The first had contemplated having a large party of <u>andartes</u> seize a train which would be halted on the viaduct while the guards were overpowered and the demolition charges laid. This plan was discarded as impractical since the seizing of the train would undoubtedly alert both the bridge guards and a battalion of troops stationed nearby.

It will be recalled that Asopos had been ruled out at the time of the first major sabotage operation because of the seeming impossibility of approaching it from the west. A second plan sought to solve this problem by making the approach from open country which lay to the east. This method would require a strong force of <u>andartes</u>, but Aris had agreed to furnish up to a thousand men for the purpose. With the sub-

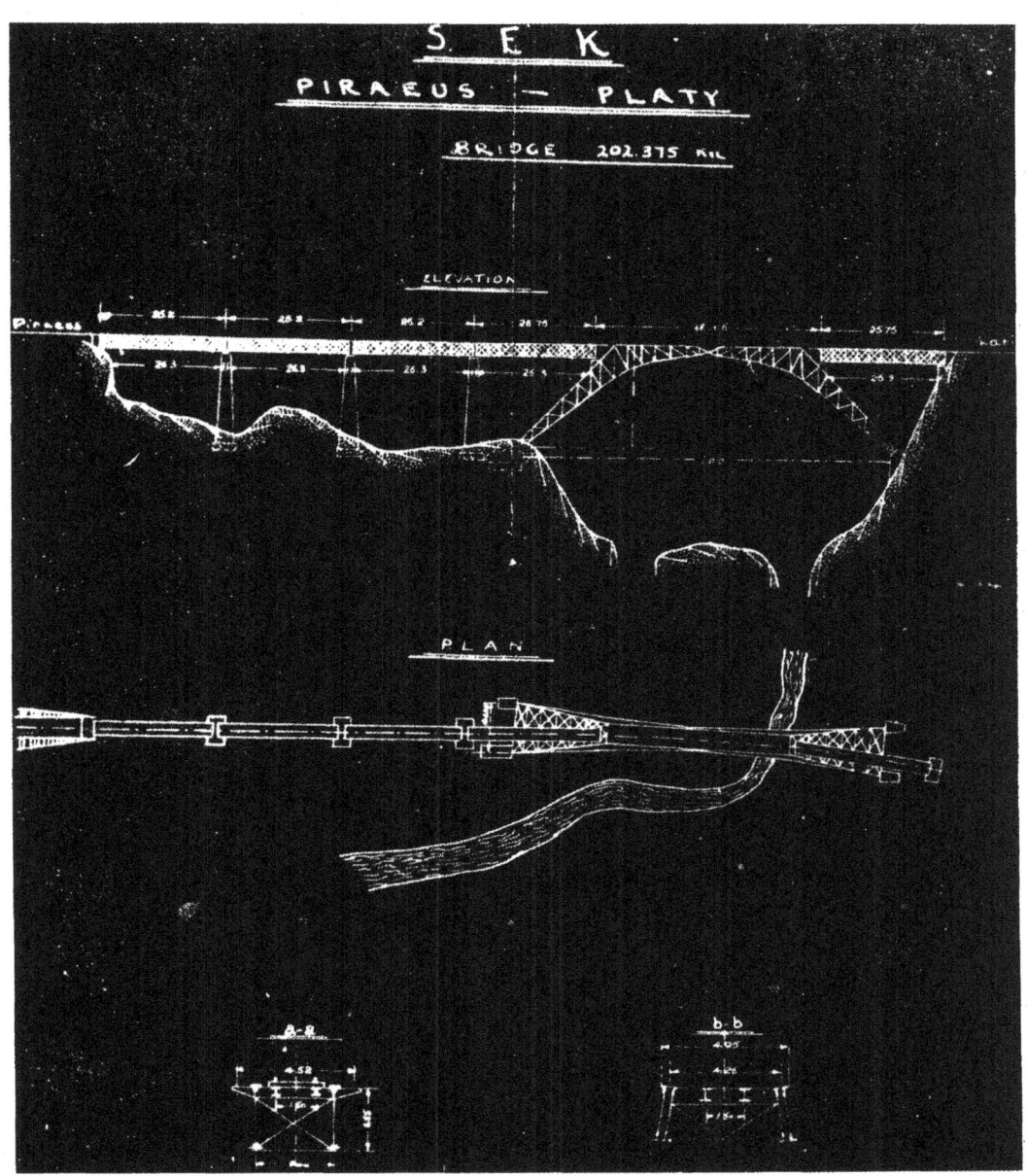

Side Elevation of ASOPOS Viaduct
(Reproduction of a blueprint used
in planning the sabotage operation)

Courtesy of the War History Branch
Department of Internal Affairs,
New Zealand Government.

sequent refusal of GHQ, ELAS to participate, this plan, too, had to be abandoned.

The third plan, and the one that was actually put into operation, called for an approach from the west by a small party which would work its way down the almost impassable gorge. Although there was little hope that the approach and setting of charges would go unobserved, it appeared to offer the only possible chance.

Three specially trained demolitions officers were parachuted in to work with the BLO's already in the area. After a final reconnaissance completed on 21 May, they were ready to undertake the venture. Securely wrapping their explosives in waterproof packs, a party of four officers and two NCO's made their way down the gorge. A number of large waterfalls and deep pools were encountered, necessitating the use of ropes to work the men and their packs around the obstacles. After two back-breaking days they had progressed to a point about a quarter of a mile above the viaduct when they ran out of rope. Faced by obstacles that could not be negotiated without extensive use of rope ladders and slings they were forced to halt. The explosives were cached in a dry place and the BLO's returned to their headquarters in Anatoli to request and await an air drop of additional rope.

Postponing the operation until the next full moon, the group did not set out again until mid-June. Retracing their steps a six-man team reached a point almost under the bridge late on the night of 19 June. The following day, making observation from hidden positions, they noted that repairs were being effected and that scaffolding had been erected around the piers supporting the main span. On the night of the 20th, after sending back the two NCO's with instructions to get a hot meal ready, the four officers advanced toward the pier supporting the northern brace of the main span. They were pleased to discover that the men working on the bridge had not only opened a path through the barbed wire around the pier, but also had left a ladder which took the BLO's up through the scaffolding where charges could be most effectively placed.

Two men clambered up to place the charges while the other two stood guard. During the one-hour period that the task required, only one sentry approached. He was knocked out by a well-placed blow with a blackjack and dropped into the gorge below. Shortly after midnight, the job was completed -- 90-minute fuses were set and the group retreated back up the gorge. A few minutes after 2 a.m. on 21 June the charges detonated and the entire main span dropped 200 feet into the gorge below.

Although the Germans had guarded both ends of the viaduct, they had been so confident that it would be impossible for anyone to approach down the gorge, that route had been left unguarded. Even after the destruction of the viaduct the German command apparently did not consider the possibility that the saboteurs had come down the Asopos gorge. Convinced that the destruction had been an act of treachery, the entire guard detail was condemned to death. The BLO's returned to Anatoli safely.

In spite of the fact that ELAS had refused to render direct assistance in the Asopos operation, the BLO's realized that they could not have approached the viaduct or returned safely if the surrounding

ASOPOS Viaduct -- 23 June
Dropped span and wreckage of cantilever support

ASOPOS Viaduct -- 2 July
Debris cleared for erection of south end
emergency supports

ASOPOS Viaduct -- 15 July
Repairs in progress.
New supports being constructed at north end

ASOPOS Viaduct -- 26 July
Over a month after the sabotage operation.
Repairs still incomplete.

area had not been under firm _andarte_ control.

A bridge engineering expert, flown in from Germany to supervise the repair work on Asopos, predicted that he would have the job done in six weeks. Five weeks later as the almost-completed framework of the superstructure was being anchored into place, the whole thing collapsed killing the engineer and about forty workmen. Another engineer completed the job but not until the railway had been cut for ten weeks.[16]

## Widespread Sabotage

Starting with the destruction of the Asopos viaduct a wave of sabotage swept over Greece. The thirty BLO's who now constituted the BMM were active in organizing, directing, and conducting the sabotage campaign. Some of the BLO's acted as independent demolitions teams, hastening from one operation to another. Others worked closely with _andarte_ bands, directing their activities along profitable lines.

Major and minor acts of destructive violence and harassment hamstrung the German and Italian supply lines. Signal communications, except for radio, broke down completely as telephone and telegraph lines all over the country were cut and repair parties annihilated.

In the Mount Olympus area, on the highway between Larisa and Kozani, the Sarandoporou pass was blocked and kept closed for two weeks. A strong force of two German battalions was required to force a passage to reopen the road. In addition, the railway line between Larisa and Salonika was cut in many place on successive days, causing innumerable delays and disruptions of service.

In Thessaly and Epirus, a 50-mile stretch of highway between Kalabaka and Ioannina was systematically destroyed. Under the supervision of BLO's, ELAS bands in the east and EDES bands in the west blew every culvert and bridge on the main east-west road. Where there were no bridges or culverts, huge sections of cliff were dynamited to pile tons of rock and earth on the road. In other places the embankments were cut away, dropping sections of the road into the gorges below.

In southern Epirus, EDES forces cut the Agrinion-Arta road and denied its use to the enemy for several weeks. Efforts to reopen the highway or to force convoys through were staunchly resisted with heavy casualties being inflicted on both German and Italian units. Farther south, an important bridge on the road from Agrinion to Athens was completely destroyed.

In the Peloponnesus and eastern Roumeli, results were less satisfactory, although a BLO and a band of andartes in the latter region did succeed in blowing up a railroad bridge as a train passed over it. Enemy personnel losses were heavy and the rail line was disrupted for many weeks.

Because of its strategic location as a possible Allied invasion area, the Peloponnesus was heavily garrisoned and the occupation forces were able to maintain control. Another factor also militated against the conduct of successful sabotage campaign in that region. ELAS forces chose this time to attack the newly formed monarchist ES and EOA guerrilla bands. As a result, instead of an intensified campaign of sabotage directed at the forces of the occupation, most of the Peloponnesus guerrilla activity was confined to internecine strife between monarchist and ELAS guerrillas.

The _andarte_ forces were not able to put aside jealousies and rivalries even for the short period of the sabotage campaign. On 21 June, the opening day of operations, an EDES band moved into northern Epirus to conduct demolitions operations. Since ELAS claimed that territory, General Sarafis lodged an immediate complaint with Woodhouse, threatening to send strong ELAS forces from Macedonia and Thessaly to drive the intruders out. Woodhouse admitted some personal guilt in the matter, explaining that he had encouraged EDES to make the move as there were important installations in the area which should be neutralized. Sarafis indignantly replied that ELAS forces in northern Epirus were capable of conducting the operations and would do so. Since this spurring on of ELAS was undoubtedly the reaction for which Woodhouse was hoping, he agreed to have the EDES band recalled.

Hardly had this incident been settled, when the BMM headquarters was informed by the BLO in Roumeli that ELAS bands had attacked EKKA and inflicted casualties. Since GHQ, ELAS had agreed not to molest EKKA after Psaros' last capture, this was a flagrant breach of faith for which Sarafis admitted ELAS was to blame. He explained, as in the previous cases, that it was all a mistake -- the attack had occurred while Aris was absent from the Roumeli district. In extenuation, Sarafis maintained that the poorly equipped Roumeli ELAS bands had been tempted beyond their powers to resist by the large quantities of weapons which the British had recently furnished EKKA.

On the whole, however, the campaign was highly successful. To cope with the emergency, two additional German divisions were moved into Greece and were thus kept from employment on other fronts. So completely disrupted were the enemy's transportation facilities, that German soldiers captured in Epirus said that it had taken them seventeen days to make the trip from Athens -- a distance of about 200 miles as the crow flies.

The inevitable reprisals followed swiftly. Excerpts from official German Army reports show such entries as the following:

> 2 July 1943 -- 4 villages burned down and 50 Communists shot near Litochoron [Litokhoron] for attack on German sergeant and blasting of railroad tracks.
>
> 4 July 1943 -- 87 suspects shot while trying to escape.
>
> 5 July 1943 -- 50 Greeks shot in Melaxa for sabotage of cable lines.[17]

On 11 July, the BMM received word that the landings in Sicily had been accomplished. Word was immediately flashed to the guerrilla bands throughout Greece and the widespread wave of violence stopped almost as suddenly as it had begun.

### The National Bands Agreement Signed

Shortly after the attack on EKKA a representative from the EAM Central Committee arrived in Roumeli to report that the National Bands Agreement -- which EAM/ELAS referred to as "The Military Agreement" -- had been approved. In its final amended form, the agreement retained much of the original as far as principles of organization and rights of individual _andartes_ and bands were concerned. However, instead of giving the BLO's broad powers of direction and control, it called for the establishment of a joint BMM and _andarte_ headquarters to be known as the Joint General Headquarters which would exercise control under the over-all direction of the Middle East Command. While the agreement recognized the presence of the BMM as representing the Middle East Command, the powers of control and direction given the BLO's in the original version were now reserved to the Joint General Headquarters (JGHQ).[18] On 5 July, the agreement was signed at Kalabaka with Brigadier Myers signing for the Middle East Command; Sarafis, Aris, and Tzimas for EAM/ELAS.

With ELAS pledged to support guerrilla unification, the BMM anticipated no difficulties in persuading all other andarte organizations to sign the National Bands Agreement. Zervas, however, turned balky and refused to accept the amended version, saying that he preferred the original which he had already signed some months previously. He was, he added, violently opposed to the establishment of a joint headquarters which would give ELAS three votes to his one. Eventually, after much argument and persuasion, in which it was impressed on Zervas that the C-in-C, Middle East particularly desired his concurrence, the EDES leader reluctantly put his name to the document.

News of the signing of the agreement was promptly forwarded to Cairo and, a few days later, an announcement was broadcast by GHQ, Middle East:

> It is therefore now an accomplished fact that all Greek andarte bands, irrespective of their political or other tendencies have been welded into a united and co-ordinated instrument for the furtherance of the Allied struggle.[19]

## Establishment of the Joint General Headquarters

As in the case of the well-known dilemma of Mohammed in regard to the mountain, since ELAS refused to send a responsible officer to the Joint General Headquarters, Brigadier Myers went to Pertouli, establishing the joint headquarters with GHQ, ELAS.

On 18 July 1943 the first joint session was opened with Brigadier Myers reading a message from General Sir Henry Maitland Wilson congratulating the Greek _andartes_ on their diversionary sabotage efforts during the Allied invasion of Sicily. Myers also announced that the C-in-C advised the BMM and the _andarte_ force to remain quiet for the next few months and devote their time to recruiting, training, and re-equipping. Guerrilla activities should be restricted to defensive operations and such attacks as might be deemed necessary to sustain interest and to train recruits. Meanwhile, the BMM would supervise training, requisition and distribute supplies, as well as develop long-range plans for guerrilla co-operation in the contemplated Allied invasion of Greece.

While the conference was still in session, Colonel Psaros and an EKKA delegation arrived. In spite of the fact that relations between ELAS and EKKA had been far from happy, Colonel Psaros met Sarafis, Aris, and Tzimas without visible enmity and, after some discussion of common goals and aims, it was mutually agreed that the two organizations would thenceforth work in harmony. In a subsequent meeting with the BMM chief, after being promised large quantities of weapons and other supplies, Psaros signed the National Bands Agreement on behalf of EKKA.

On or about 20 July, all BLO's met at Pertouli for the first general conference since the BMM had begun operations in Greece. The latest requirements of the Middle East Command were explained to the liaison officers and suggestions for implementation were discussed. Of primary importance in the order of business was the matter of the attitude of the Italian occupation forces. Mussolini was slipping and the Italians, never very enthusiastic about the war, could read the handwriting on the wall. Some surrender feelers had already been put out by Italian commanders in Greece and Myers advised the BLO's that they were authorized by SOE Cairo to negotiate and accept the surrender of Italian units.

Toward the end of July, during the course of a visit to JGHQ, Zervas expressed his disappointment at Myers having located his headquarters with the "Communists." He was fearful of the future intentions of EAM/ELAS and strongly advocated that the British discontinue all support to that organization. Myers refused to consider cutting off aid to ELAS but assured Zervas that supplies to EDES would continue. Brigadier Myers' decision to continue support of ELAS was not dictated by personal preference, as he was equally apprehensive of the ultimate goals of EAM/ELAS which he was now convinced was Communist-dominated. He was, however, well aware that he could not accomplish his assigned missions without the co-operation of ELAS.

At that time, ELAS controlled some four-fifths of mainland Greece while EDES was almost completely confined to the comparatively small area of Epirus. The British estimated that guerrilla strength had risen to well over twenty thousand. ELAS had nearly sixteen thousand members in active bands and approximately the same number in its town and village reserve units. EDES had less than a third of the ELAS total, with only about five thousand active andartes and an equal number of reservists. EKKA had enrolled only a few hundred, although it was growing and was destined to reach a total of nearly a thousand within a few weeks.

The 29 July meeting of the JGHQ, which Zervas attended, passed several resolutions supplementing the provisions of the National Bands Agreement. These established the right of EDES to recruit within ELAS territory and a like privilege for ELAS to form new bands in areas controlled by EDES. The BMM also agreed to pay the guerrilla forces one pound per month in gold for each member, exclusive of the reserves. Territorial rights in several disputed areas were settled and a joint commission was formed to investigate and resolve differences for areas where no immediate decision could be reached. A conciliatory spirit seemed to prevail throughout the discussion and it appeared that the National Bands Agreement might be the means of resolving all former differences.

It soon appeared, however, that the amicable relationship was only an illusion. Although the agreement had now been signed by all major guerrilla organizations and their leaders had apparently reached an understanding, clashes between EDES and ELAS continued. EDES was determined to enlarge its sphere of influence and ELAS was equally determined to prevent not only the expansion of EDES but also of all other guerrilla movements. The BLO's were continually on the move, going from one area to another seeking to effect compromises between rival band leaders and put an end to Greek versus Greek conflict. Brigadier Myers, in describing the uneasy situation which existed in the mountains of Greece, says:

> The moment EAM/ELAS were given an opportunity to carry out an act of aggression against another organization out of sight of a British officer, they would do so, rather than attack the enemy. On the other hand, to be fair to EAM, it should be added that, as soon as the back of the British officers were turned, some of their lower level rivals in EDES, knowing they could count on our moral support, seldom missed an opportunity of tormenting ELAS into such acts of aggression.[20]

In settling quarrels between bands, the BLO's continued to hold their trump card -- the supply channel. Bands guilty of instigating clashes could be controlled by cancelling air drops to their area. Unfortunately, the thirty or forty BLO's which then composed the BMM were too few to be really effective in policing the mountains of Greece or acting as referees between contending bands. Cairo was notified that the strength of the BMM would have to be doubled and the number of radios proportionately increased.

## Politics and the Neraidha Airstrip

All efforts of the BMM to remain aloof from politics were unavailing; as widespread internecine strife developed, it became increasingly difficult to avoid involvement in the Greek national pastime. Not only was there the immediate problem of conflict between guerrilla factions due to ideological differences, but there was also the problem with which the resistance organizations were concerned, the government of Greece after liberation. The resistance organizations, particularly EAM, demanded assurances that Britain would not force Greece to accept the monarchy when the war was over. Brigadier Myers had sent innumerable messages to SOE Cairo outlining the political problems in which the BMM had become involved and warning of the possibility of civil war developing. The authorities in Cairo were not convinced that politics were being thrust upon the BMM and looked with jaundiced eye on a military mission becoming involved in the hopeless maze of Greek politics. Replies to Myers' messages broadly hinted that it would be better if the BMM and the guerrillas would confine their activities to fighting the war and not concern themselves with matters best left to the Foreign Office and heads of government.

After vainly attempting to explain the situation in radios to the Middle East Command, in June Brigadier Myers requested permission to visit Cairo for a comprehensive discussion of his political problems. He suggested that arrangements be made to get him out of Greece via one of the Greek fishing boats, known as caiques, which regularly ran the German coastal blockades. Cairo replied that his method of exfiltration was much too risky and made a countersuggestion that he could be flown out if an airfield could be prepared. Myers agreed to see what could be done, bearing in mind that a landing field would also make the infiltration of officers and bulky equipment much easier and safer.

In the spring of 1943, Captain Denys Hamson had been assigned to western Thessaly as senior liaison officer to work with Karageorgis, the EAM representative in that area, and an ELAS band leader named Itamos. Because there were no other guerrilla bands in the vicinity and Itamos did not have to concern himself with wiping out competition, he devoted his full energies to co-operating with the BLO. As a consequence, although Hamson was bitter toward ELAS because it had earlier broken up the Vlakhos band to which he had been assigned, he managed to get along well with Itamos.

With the help of the guerrilla leader an excellent drop zone was established near the village of Neraidha, a few miles southwest of Kardhitsa. The site selected was a fairly broad plateau located at an altitude of about 2,600 feet. The senior BLO and his assistants established comfortable quarters in the unused summer villa of General Plastiras which overlooked the drop zone. A group of villagers were trained in drop recovery and not only assisted in the reception of large quantities of supplies, but also met several new BLO's who were parachuted to the plateau. Between drops, the BLO's made trips into the mountains checking on distribution of supplies and inspecting guerrilla training.

On one occasion when a drop was expected, the signal fires attracted enemy attention and served as an excellent bombing target. Several of the drop crew were seriously wounded. Thereafter, arrangements were made with SOE Cairo for the use of a signal code. Each month a 30-word sentence was transmitted from Cairo and the pilot would flash the letter for the day on his first pass over the drop zone. The drop zone fires would not be lit until the proper signal had been received. There was no further trouble with signal fires pinpointing the field as a target for enemy bombers.

In late June, when Cairo suggested the construction of an airstrip, the drop zone at Neraidha was selected as the best location. Necessary supplies, including funds to pay laborers, began arriving in July. The requirement established by SOE Cairo was for a strip 200 yards wide and 1700 yards long which, it was estimated, would take about one month to complete. Using his trained drop-receiving crew as foremen, Captain Hamson employed as many as 700 men and women as well as over 50 ox and mule carts in a two-shift, dawn-till-dark operation.

Every precaution was taken to preserve the secrecy of the airstrip construction and Itamos provided a detachment of 250 andartes to serve as security guards in the surrounding mountains. All laborers were required to live at the site of the strip and were not permitted to visit or return to their homes while the work was in progress. In order to prevent large amounts of gold from appearing in the region and arousing enemy suspicion, agents were sent to distant towns and cities to convert gold to Greek currency on the blackmarket. In spite of these precautions, a large proportion of the countryside must have been well aware that something big was in the making. the BLO's, however, had confidence in the loyalty of the Greek mountain people and were also reasonably certain that rumors which might reach the occupation forces would be so wildly exaggerated as to be completely unbelievable.

Although the andartes seldom took prisoners, on one occasion an overambitious guerrilla brought a captured German sergeant to the Nerhaidha airstrip for interrogation by the BLO's. This was a most serious breach of security and, fearful that the German might escape or be rescued, the senior BLO reluctantly ordered the man's captor to take his prisoner out in the woods and shoot him.

This was not the only case in which the BLO's were forced to order or condone the shooting of prisoners or spies. Both the Germans and Italians sent many spies into the mountains, some of them collaborating Greeks and others soldiers who claimed to be deserters. While some of them may have been bona fide deserters, the BMM and the andartes could not afford to take chances. A brief interrogation usually uncovered the true reasons for the presence of any stranger in the mountains -- the andartes were invariably well-informed -- and the spies were quickly disposed of. Among the most ingenious schemes for infiltrating an espionage agent into JGHQ involved a Greek peddler who was possibly innocent of traitorous intent. The itinerant vendor of blackmarket luxuries who had made several previous visits to the headquarters showed up one day with three attractive young women, saying that they were furnished for the "recreation" of the BLO's. A check soon showed that all three had been extremely friendly with the Italian garrison in their home town and evidence indicated that one was quite definitely a spy. She was shot and the others were kept in custody in a mountain village for the duration of the war, where they undoubtedly led a useful existence providing for the recreation of nearby andartes. Espionage never developed into a serious problem in the mountains of Greece.

As clearing and leveling of the airstrip progressed, Hamson realized that enemy air observation could easily detect and identify the project and an elaborate camouflage operation was undertaken. The straight borders of the field were broken up by irregular clearings, lines of pine boughs were laid along filled-in ditches to give them the appearance of streams, and several hundred pine trees were carted from the surrounding hills and their sharpened butts stuck into the cleared areas. So successful was the camouflage that the Middle East Air Force, which photographed the field shortly before its completion, radioed that interpretation of photos showed the strip to be unusable. Upon receipt of a sharp reply from Brigadier Myers, who had closely inspected the field, the air force agreed to have a pilot parachuted into the area to inspect the job on the ground.

On 4 August, several days before the first plane was expected, the pilot arrived and gave the airstrip his unqualified approval, remarking that a lot of unnecessary work had been performed. The DC-3's which would be using the field were capable of landing and taking off in 600 yards; the 1,700-yard length of the Neraidha strip was, therefore, far longer than the air force required. It appeared that SOE Cairo had made a slight error, possibly attributable to one of its many changes and reorganizations. Had the proper information been furnished, the airstrip would have been completed with a much smaller expenditure of manpower, money, and time.

With the Neraidha airstrip all but operational, Brigadier Myers prepared for his trip to Cairo on which he was to be accompanied by representatives of the Greek guerrilla forces who also wished to confer with the British authorities and the Greek Government-in-Exile. On the night of 9 August the first plane landed, discharged passengers and cargo, loaded passengers, and departed -- all within a matter of minutes. Disembarked passengers included six new BLO's and with them came several additional radios. The planned passenger list for the trip to Cairo included Brigadier Myers, Andreas Tzimas of EAM/ELAS, Kominus Pyramaglou of EDES, and George Kartalis of EKKA. At the last minute, Tzimas introduced three members of the EAM Central Committee and insisted that they also accompany the party. Aware that at least two of the three EAM delegates were Communists, and although reluctant to give KKE such a preponderance of representation, Myers was obliged to consent to their inclusion. Tzimas flatly refusing to go to Cairo or take part in the conference unless the EAM delegates were included.

Also among the embarking passengers was Captain Denys Hamson, who had finally solved his own evacuation problem. It would appear that his enthusiastic pushing of the airstrip project had not been generated entirely by his devotion to the cause of Greek resistance.

CHAPTER IV

REORGANIZATIONS AND REPRISALS
(1943 - 1944)

## Reorganization of German Forces

During 1941 and most of 1942, German forces in Greece were drastically reduced by transfers to other and more active theaters. As 1942 drew to a close, except for small garrison units in the vicinities of Athens and Salonika and on a few key islands, the only major concentration of German troops was the 22d Airborne Division, on the island of Crete.

In December 1942, the 11th Luftwaffe Field Division was sent to Greece to replace the 22d Airborne but, because of widespread unrest as evidenced by intensified guerrilla activity, it was determined to retain both divisions.[1] The 11th Luftwaffe Division, instead of going on to Crete, took over the maintenance of law and order in the Attica region, north of Athens.

As a result of Allied successes in Africa and a loss of confidence in their Italian allies, in mid-1943 the Germans began a build-up of their forces in Greece. The German High Command was concerned with the possibility of an Allied invasion of Greece and for this reason strength was concentrated on Crete, in the Peloponnesus, and along the western coast. In the Peloponnesus, the LXVIII Corps was established with the 1st Panzer and 117th Light Infantry Divisions. At the end of June, the 1st Mountain Division was brought to Epirus from Albania. Strengthening of the Salonika area was accomplished by increasing the number of Bulgarian units -- most of which would come under German command in the event of invasion. As German units arrived in Italian occupation areas, they were used to bolster the established garrisons and came under Italian tactical control.

On 26 July 1943, Directive No. 48, issued by the German High Command, centralized the defense of the Balkans under Field Marshal Maximilian von Weichs. As Commander-in-Chief, Southeast, von Weichs' mission was to prepare for a possible Allied invasion from Africa or Italy. Coastal defenses were to be built and, to protect rear area lines of communications, the guerrilla menace was to be eliminated throughout the southeast theater. A third task, which came as a result of the resignation of Mussolini, was to make preparations for taking over from the Italians in the event of the complete collapse of the Germans' wavering ally. The Southeast Command placed General Alexander Loehr, command Army Group E, in control of German forces in Greece.[2]

In general, Italian counterguerrilla measures had been ineffectual and had served to encourage rather than inhibit Greek resistance. The Italians had little stomach for pursuing the elusive andartes through the mountains and even a moderate show of resistance generally discouraged punitive expeditions. Reprisals were restricted to burning small, undefended villages and the imprisonment or shooting of a few hostages. The German troops which were brought in to bolster the Italian garrisons were an entirely different proposition and the andartes soon found that they could no longer commit sabotage or waylay patrols with virtual impunity.

One of the first rude awakenings came as ELAS bands in the Grammos Mountains of northern Epirus prepared a welcome for an advance element of the 1st Mountain Division as it moved south from Albania. Although the action took place in Albania, it was in a region in which the borders were not clearly defined and the guerrilla units involved were predominantly Greek. Thinking to inflict serious losses and a major defeat on the Germans before they could get organized in the region, an ambush was prepared.[3]

Using tactics which had been successful against the Italians, the ELAS force took over the town of Leskovic and moved all residents into the surrounding hills. Placing men in houses along the main street, the andarte leader planned to let the advance guard pass through the town and then open fire on the main body while it was confined within the narrow limits of the street. A large body of andartes, hidden in the nearby hills, would close in to complete the destruction of the German force.

Instead of marching blindly into the trap, on approaching Leskovic the advance guard executed a double envelopment, sending flankers to both sides of the town. Confused by the movement, some of the andartes opened fire on the flanking parties before the main body was in range. Warned by the shots, the Germans quickly surrounded the town and subjected it to a heavy concentration of artillery fire. A counterattack by the andarte reserve force was beaten off and the Germans launched an assault against the partially destroyed town, cleaning out the guerrillas in house-to-house fighting. Still comparatively inexperienced in guerrilla fighting, the mountain troops permitted a number of what they thought were civilians to flee during the engagement. Later they learned that none of their opponents had been uniformed and that the "civilians" they had permitted to escape were actually guerrilla combatants.

Reorganization of the Guerrilla Forces

As the Germans reorganized to improve the defenses of Greece, ELAS also effected a major reorganization of its forces. GHQ, ELAS issued an order fixing 1 September 1943 as the date by which all ELAS area headquarters and forces would be redesignated as regular military units. Macedonia Headquarters was renamed the 9th Western Macedonia Division, Thessaly Headquarters became the 1st Thessaly Division, Epirus General Command the 8th Epirus Division, and Roumeli General Command, the 13th Central Greece Division. By order of the ELAS Central Command in Athens, the Peloponnesus General Command was redesignated the 3d Division. Under each division, bands were to be reorganized as regiments, battalions, and companies.[4] These military designations were, of course, just terms of convenience as the ELAS forces totaled less than half of the fifty to sixty thousand men which a strength of five divisions would imply.

The EDES field force also entered upon a period of reorganization which involved a change of name. For some time, relations between Zervas and the EDES resistance organization in Athens had grown increasingly strained. Zervas, presumably at the instigation of the BMM, had sent messages of loyalty to the Greek king and Government-in-Exile. There is some question whether the sentiments expressed in these broadcast messages reflected Zervas' personal feelings or were politically expedient propaganda. To the EDES of Athens, however, it appeared that Zervas had rejected his former republicanism and gone over to the monarchist camp. Further widening the rift between the two factions were well substantiated rumors that the group in Athens was involved in collaborationist activity, co-operating with the puppet government as well as the occupation authorities.[5]

Relations between the Athens EDES and the field EDES reached the breaking point on 23 July 1943 when Zervas officially changed the name of his guerrilla force to Ethniki Organosis Ellinikon Andarton (Greek Nationalist Guerrilla Units).[6] Although the new designation had been suggested by the BMM and the initials EOEA were occasionally used, the new name never became popular and even the British continued to refer to Zervas' force as EDES.[7]

The military EDES, or EOEA, was reorganized during the summer of 1943 into eight or ten units, with two regiments of two battalions in each unit. Here again, the military designations were a matter of convenience rather than an indication of size, as the EDES strength of five to seven thousand would permit each battalion to number only 125 to 175 men.

The Italian Surrender

Throughout the month of August, speculation on a possible Italian surrender was rife. Individual Italian commanders had approached BLO's and guerrilla leaders with surrender feelers and a number of deserters had actually joined the andarte bands. On 3 September the matter finally came to a head when the Italian Government signed an armistice with the Allies. Although most of the Italian units in Greece surrendered to the Germans, the Pinerolo Division and the Aosta Cavalry Regiment, which had garrisoned Thessaly, capitulated to JGHQ.

Under the terms of the surrender, those Italian soldiers who wished to fight against their former allies were to be enrolled in self-contained units of company or battalion size, which would be incorporated into larger ELAS forces. It was understood that all such units would later be combined into one Italian force and assigned an operational area. Those who did not wish to fight were disarmed and placed in POW camps. The BMM agreed to support all prisoners and would also provide payment for those who joined the andarte ranks at the same rate as that provided for the Greek andartes -- one pound per month per man. General Infante, commander of the Pinerolo Division, was required to establish his headquarters with JGHQ and issue orders to his units from Pertouli.[8]

Since the two Italian units were in ELAS territory at the time of their surrender, that organization promptly pre-empted all surplus Italian armament. The Germans, enraged at the Italian defection dispatched strong forces which attempted to prevent the equipment of the Pinerolo Division and the Aosta Cavalry from falling into andarte hands. ELAS, however, had foreseen this contingency and all captured equipment, including a number of artillery pieces, was rushed into guerrilla strongholds in the Pindus Mountains.

EDES made strong representations to JGHQ in an effort to gain a share of the booty but, while ELAS kindly offered to turn over large numbers of unarmed Italian soldiers, EDES' pleas for trucks and weapons were ignored. EDES did obtain some equipment by disarming small Italian units in Epirus and also gained quantities of small arms from Italian soldiers who sold their weapons before surrendering to the Germans. So serious did the arms-selling traffic become that the Germans announced that any Italian surrendering without his weapon would be summarily shot. While this ruling undoubtedly induced some Italians to retain their weapons, it also had the effect of driving many of those who had already disposed of them to take refuge with the andartes.

The huge amount of additional equipment and armament acquired by ELAS enabled them to form the 16th Thessaly Division and the 5th Attica-Euboea Brigade.

## Formation of the Allied Military Mission

About the middle of September, the delegation of resistance and guerrilla leaders returned from Cairo. On the plane were also several American officers who were to act in a liaison capacity in conjunction with the BMM, which was now redesignated as the Allied Military Mission, or AMM. Individual liaison officers would henceforth be referred to as ALO's rather than BLO's. Brigadier Myers did not return to Greece and permanent command of the AMM passed to Woodhouse, now a lieutenant colonel. The placing of Woodhouse in command of the AMM did not please Sarafis who, as a regular officer, had little regard for those he termed "wartime" officers. In addition, he also feared that the change would not benefit EAM/ELAS since he felt Brigadier Myers had shown less bias against his organization than had Woodhouse.[9]

## The Pinerolo Division Dissolved

Meanwhile, the German forces were experiencing serious difficulties in taking over a number of islands that had been garrisoned by the Italians. In the Ionian Sea, the islands of Corfu and Cephalonia were being staunchly defended by the Italians and in the Aegean a number of islands had been reinforced by the British and were also refusing to capitulate. To divert the attention of the Germans from the disputed islands, SOE Cairo called for another wave of widespread guerrilla activity in Greece. Disruption of communications by cutting telephone and telegraph lines was to be followed by attacks on airfields.

Although most of the designated airfields were in the western part of the country, one was located at Larisa, in Thessaly, and SOE Cairo suggested that the Pinerolo Division make the attack. General Infante held that the disintegration of his division precluded making an open attack on the German garrison of Larisa but did agree to form a small unit of volunteers to infiltrate the airfield and destroy aircraft. In spite of the fact that the volunteer force was accompanied by several ALO's and a number of ELAS <u>andartes</u>, the mission was a complete and abject failure. The group of volunteers not only withdrew without destroying any planes, but also abandoned all its demolitions. These the Germans found the next day and the only result of the abortive attack was a prompt and severe reprisal by the Germans in which the Germans destroyed a nearby village of two hundred homes.[10]

ELAS placed the entire blame for the fiasco on the Italians and, highly dissatisfied with this as well as other exhibitions of Italian ineptitude in the art of guerrilla warfare, announced its intention of disarming the entire division. The AMM voiced strong disapproval and persuaded ELAS not to carry out the threatened action.

With Italy's declaration of war against Germany on 13 October, General Infante asked that, in accordance with the terms of surrender, his division be reformed and given a definite sector in which to conduct operations against the Germans. On the morning of 14 October, GHQ, ELAS agreed to his request and, in the afternoon, quietly rounded up all Italian units and disarmed them.[11] A few Italian soldiers who volunteered to fight with the andartes were accepted into ELAS units as individuals. The considerable quantities of additional equipment thus acquired, including horses from the Aosta Cavalry Regiment, enabled ELAS to form a cavalry brigade as well as a field artillery battery and a mountain artillery unit.

## Fighting between EDES and ELAS

In mid-October large-scale fighting broke out between EDES and the ELAS 8th Epirus Division. Charges and countercharges flew thick and fast with bothe EDES and ELAS accusing the other of fomenting the conflict and also of collaborating with the enemy. Sarafis claimed that the ELAS forces would not have initiated the Epirus conflict since the 8th Division, with a strength of only two thousand, was the only ELAS unit in an area where there were very much stronger EDES forces.[12] Colonel Woodhouse, speaking for the Middle East Command, made no secret of where the British placed the blame for the outbreak of internecine strife and the rift between the AMM and EAM/ELAS widened when he notified GHQ, ELAS that there would be no further air drops until fighting between the two <u>andarte</u> organizations stopped.[13] Sarafis apparently understood this to apply to EDES as well as to ELAS and, when the British continued to supply Zervas, the ELAS commander was greatly incensed at what he considered a breach of faith.

To aid the 8th Division in its fight against EDES, Aris immediately formed an expeditionary force, composed of all personnel from the ELAS Training School for Officers and a unit of the 13th Thessaly Division. As he moved west with his reinforcing group, another ELAS force from Macedonia was sent south to attack EDES on its northern flank.

With civil war raging in the mountains, the Germans began a major campaign to open the principal highways and clean out the guerrilla bands which had blocked some of them for months. Faced with the possibility of a two-front fight, Aris promptly withdrew to the south where he began the formation of a command known as GHQ/Epirus Team. Under the new command was the ELAS 8th Division as well as Aris' original expeditionary force.

## German Highway Opening Operations

In spite of difficulties occasioned by the Italian surrender, the augmented and reorganized German forces made progress in preparing for the defense of Greece. Work on air bases and coastal defenses was performed by labor battalions largely composed of Italian POW's, while German troop units conducted operations against the guerrillas.

In conjunction with the Bulgarian units, the Edessa-Florina road, in northern Macedonia, was cleared of guerrillas without encountering serious opposition. Operation PANTHER, a much more ambitious project, was begun in October with the object of reopening the principal highways in Thessaly and Epirus. At the conclusion of the operation in early November, the east-west route from Larisa through the Metsovon Pass to Ioannina was open as was the north-south highway from Ioannina to Arta.

GHQ, ELAS and JGHQ had been forced to abandon Pertouli and the ELAS military organization, split by German drives across Central Greece, was almost completely disrupted. Although heavy losses were inflicted on the guerrillas, the Germans lacked the numerical strength to maintain complete control of the areas they had re-opened. In typical guerrilla fashion the andarte bands, which had fled in the face of strong German forces, returned as soon as the enemy troops retired from the mountain areas.

One of the factors contributing to the success of Operation PANTHER was the secrecy with which German preparations were conducted. This was one of the few occasions on which the andartes were caught completely off guard. The Germans estimated that Operation PANTHER had accounted for the deaths of 1,400 andartes and their supporters. It is probable, however, that the total included more supporters than actual andarte fighting men. Because guerrilla units, particularly ELAS, were seldom uniformed the Germans were inclined to identify all male civilians as guerrillas. Sarafis claimed that German casualties totaled 1,000 and that ELAS losses were only 500 killed, wounded, and missing.[14]

## Counterguerrilla Security Measures

To protect military traffic and keep highways open, the Germans established strongpoints covering important structures and locations. Each strongpoint was set up as an all-around defense position, equipped with telephone or radio and with sufficient food and ammunition to enable its defenders to hold for two weeks. While a larger number of strongpoints would have expedited control, troop strength limitations made it impossible to locate them at closer than six-mile intervals. To compensate for the shortage of control points, reconnaissance patrols and well-armed motorized road patrols operated within each sector. To make it difficult for guerrillas to plan ambushes, patrols varied their schedules and formations constantly.

In addition to the strongpoint patrols, each German division formed mobile road control detachments. Equipped with armored reconnaissance cars, truck-mounted machine guns, searchlights, and 20-mm. antiaircraft guns, these platoon-strength detachments patrolled the highways day and night. They were in constant touch with division headquarters by radio and could be directed to trouble spots with a minimum of delay. However, a shortage of motor vehicles and gasoline prevented the patrol system being fully developed. As a further security measure, barrier zones were established along stretches of road particularly vulnerable to attack. Within these zones no night movement, except that of the occupation forces, was permitted. The local populace was advised that after nightfall anyone sighted on or near the barrier zones would be fired on without warning.

Sabotage of railroad lines was an almost continual occurrence, drastically reducing the traffic on the Athens-Salonika line. In an effort to protect the rail lines, a restricted zone was established on either side of the right of way. This zone which extended five kilometers on either side of the railways in country districts was reduced to two hundred meters in the cities. All persons were warned that they would be shot if found within the restricted area.

In an effort to curb the highly efficient guerrilla intelligence net, every effort was made to isolate the civilian population from the guerrillas and the German troops. A tight supervision over movements to and from towns was effected in order to prevent civilians from contacting the guerrilla bands. All persons moving in or out of the garrisoned towns were carefully screened and night movements were prevented by perimeter guards. Separation of troops from civilian inhabitants was aimed at preventing the latter from obtaining knowledge of troop movements. Officers and men were not billeted in private homes but were housed in barracks where chance remarks or unusual activity could not be so readily noted and word passed to the guerrillas. In spite of these precautions, the resistance intelligence net continued to function and the guerrillas were invariably well informed on German troop activities.

Collaborators and the Security Battalions

Throughout the occupation of Greece there were many who collaborated with the enemy, although not always to the detriment of Greece or the Allied cause. Some political figures held office and many civil servants stayed on their jobs in a sincere effort to keep the wheels of responsible government turning. Many Greeks worked in German or Italian installations -- a form of collaboration -- because they had no other way to keep themselves and their families alive. There were, of course, others -- political figures and business men, principally -- who collaborated enthusiastically for the personal gain that would accrue through co-operation with the Axis. Not fitting precisely in any of these classifications was another group of collaborators -- the members of the Security Battalions.

Following the Italian surrender in late 1943, with forces too weak to contain the fast growing guerrilla movement, Army Group E requested and received permission to raise and equip a battalion of Greek security troops. Puppet Prime Minister Ioannis Rallis, backed by Generals Gonatas and Pangalos, fell in with the German proposal and directed the organization of several such battalions. Used principally in the Peloponnesus, the Security Battalions were under the command of Colonels Plitzanopoulos and Papadhongas, both mere figureheads.

It is probable that a large percentage of the men who enlisted in the Security Battalions did so not because they were pro-German but because they were anti-Communist. Ostensibly recruited to protect peace-loving villagers from the depredations of Communist guerrillas, the battalions were more numerous in areas where ELAS was strong.

That the Greek people understood that the Security Battalion members were motivated by a desire to combat Communism rather than assist the Axis is indicated by the treatment they received after liberation. Proscribed by the Middle East Command as well as both EDES and ELAS, after Greece was freed from the German yoke many members of the battalions were imprisoned. However, as a result of subsequent Communist excesses, within a few months most of the prisoners were released and large numbers were enlisted in the newly formed National Guard and later in the Greek Army.[16]

The actual over-all strength of the Security Battalions is uncertain. Although General Sarafis claims they mustered a total of 15,000, there were probably not more than about half that number -- available evidence indicates that there were about 12 battalions of approximately 700 men each.[17]

Collaboration by Guerrilla Bands

In their conduct of counterguerrilla operations, the Germans benefitted in no small degree from the guerrilla feuds. Andartes preoccupied with fighting each other could not engage in fighting the Germans and the conflicts between the guerrilla bands often led one organization to inform against the other. In areas where internecine strife was particularly vicious, the occupation forces played one side against the other, fomenting dissension by spreading rumors and disseminating propaganda. On some occasions, guerrilla bands even entered into informal partnerships with the Germans and provided guides for punitive forces conducting operations against rival bands.

EAM/ELAS did not engage in collaborationist activities as extensively as did their rivals. The comparatively clean slate was not, however, due to high-minded idealism or devotion to the cause. The German Army, engaged in a bitter fight against the USSR, hated Communism and distrusted

Communists and would not consider negotiating with ELAS, which they labeled Communistic. In addition, by late 1943 ELAS was strong enough to carry out its campaign to eliminate all rivals without requiring assistance. It was the smaller bands which, threatened by ELAS, found it necessary to make deals and sometimes actively co-operate with the Germans in order to avoid being wiped out. EDES and other anti-Communist organizations frequently were given a choice of three courses: join ELAS; collaborate to some degree; or be destroyed.[18] Those opposed to Communism knew the Germans would not occupy Greece forever and were, therefore, only a temporary evil -- Communism would be a permanent menace. Faced by a three-pronged dilemma, although a few chose to fight to the end and some joined ELAS, a large number accepted a degree of collaboration as being the least of the evils.

Because of his later prominent position with the Greek Government, the question of whether or not Zervas actively collaborated with the Germans has been treated with great delicacy. There is, however, little doubt that he did make deals with the enemy. Sarafis accuses Zervas of closely co-operating with the occupation forces, of supplying them with guides for punitive expeditions against ELAS, and of failing to maintain a continual wave of sabotage.

General Hubert Lanz, commander of the German <u>XXII Mountain Corps</u> which occupied western Greece, states unequivocally that cease-fire arrangements were made with Zervas. He adds that efforts to make the truce official hit a snag when both the British and German higher commands refused to sanction any formal negotiations between their subordinates in Epirus. Although he does not directly involve Zervas personally, General Lanz also records that EDES forces actively cooperated with German troop units in operations against ELAS during the summer of 1944.[19] Other German sources also provide evidence of cease-fires, nonaggression pacts, and actual EDES participation in German operations against ELAS.[20]

Dr. Arthur Piske, a high-ranking civilian official of the German air force in Greece, also provides evidence that deals were made with guerrilla bands:

> In order to meet the immense requirements for timber for the many construction jobs, the construction group established special sawmills in the Peloponnesus, in Epirus, and in the Pindus Mountains northwest of Lamia and Thermopylae.
> Later the work crews were exposed to attacks by guerrillas and had to be withdrawn, although construction officials succeeded in concluding a Balkan gentlemen's agreement with the leader of the guerrillas in Epirus. The guerrilla leader was paid to transport the cut timber into the valley.[21]

Although the implication is strong that the "Balkan gentlemen's agreement" was made with Zervas, the proof is not incontrovertible as dates and precise locations are lacking and there were also ELAS bands in Epirus.

Woodhouse, chief of the AMM, defends Zervas by presenting arguments indicating that at the time of Zervas' alleged truce with the enemy, the Middle East Command had directed that the Greek guerrillas remain quiet. He points out that General Zervas was an exceedingly wily character and not above playing the Germans for fools; if he could gain a brief respite from fighting two enemies, he should not be censured provided his dealings with the enemy did not hurt the Allied cause. As a clinching argument Woodhouse notes that Zervas immediately took up the fight against the Germans when directed to do so by the British.[22]

That there were instances of collaboration, double-dealing, and the playing of both ends against the middle, in the course of the Greek resistance movement, should not come as a surprise to any student of unconventional warfare. The andartes of Greece, as irregular forces, employed irregular methods and their behavior cannot be judged by conventional standards. That the end justifies the means is a basic tenet of guerrilla warfare. There can be little doubt that, at one time or another, individual andartes and bands found it expedient to arrange temporary cease-fires, to collaborate to a greater or less degree, or actually accept employment with the occupation forces.

The Plaka Armistice

By mid-November, the Germans had concluded their large-scale road opening operations and ELAS had been badly shaken although not, as the Germans had hoped, demoralized or completely destroyed. Many bands had been scattered and the recently established ELAS military commands were almost entirely disrupted. The joint headquarters at Pertouli had been evacuated and GHQ, ELAS had moved to the south to be established at Kerasovo, just north of Karpenision. Headquarters of the AMM was set up at Viniani, several miles distant.

All pretense of observing the National Bands Agreement had ceased, the conflict between EDES and ELAS having made it obvious that there was no longer a united guerrilla movement. With the departure for Pertouli, JGHQ had been dissolved and the EDES and EKKA representatives had returned to their respective headquarters.[23] The locating of GHQ, ELAS and the AMM headquarters at some distance from each other was indicative of the strained relations between ELAS and the ALO's. Although ELAS had assisted the AMM in the move to Viniani, the ALO's no longer desired, nor were they encouraged, to establish their headquarters in close conjuction with GHQ, ELAS. The leaders of ELAS claimed they had been handicapped in their fight against the Germans by the failure of the British to supply arms and ammunition. The AMM insisted that the civil strife had been initiated by ELAS and that their preoccupation with eliminating rivals had been at least partially responsible for the success of the German counterguerrila campaign.

While GHQ, ELAS strove to regroup its units and re-establish communications with its divisions in the north, Aris and a strongly reinforced Epirus Team again attacked EDES. Zervas' force, which had also been badly mauled in the German counterguerrilla operations, was compressed by ELAS into a small section of Epirus, behind the Arakhthos River. At one time, in early December, EDES was in desperate straits, being almost out of ammunition and bottled up in a valley less than twenty miles from the sea. Only a last-minute British air drop of ammunition saved Zervas and his andartes from almost certain annihilation. The eleventh hour reprieve, however, enabled him to rally his force and not only hold off the ELAS attack but also to launch a counterattack.

Toward the end of December, the AMM made efforts to bring the two dissident groups together for the purpose of halting the civil war. The suggestion for an armistice was made to General Sarafis as one of the first official acts of Major Gerald K. Wines, the newly arrived U.S. Army representative to the AMM.[24] ELAS agreed to submit the proposal to the

EAM Central Committee in Athens. The AMM's peace-making efforts were assisted by New Year's broadcasts by King George II and Moscow Radio, both of which called upon the Greek <u>andartes</u> to cease fighting among themselves and combine against the common enemy.

With an armistice in the wind, Zervas came to the conclusion that any cease-fire agreement would include a provision holding all forces in presently occupied areas. Before the agreement could be reached and while Aris was still attempting to regroup and replenish his ammunition supplies, EDES launched an attack all along the Epirus front and succeeded in driving to the Achelous River.

GHQ, ELAS immediately directed additional reinforcements be sent to Aris and, on 26 January 1944, the Epirus Team mounted a counter-attack which resulted in driving Zervas back to the Arakhthos River.[25] On 4 February a truce was finally arranged with, as Zervas had expected, a primary EAM/ELAS condition being that all forces remain in the territory which they occupied at the time of the cease-fire. A second condition demanded by EAM/ELAS was the denouncing of all who had collaborated with the enemy or the puppet government. A third and final condition was that immediate steps be taken to form a united guerrilla army.

The requirement that collaborators be denounced was aimed at Zervas who, having already broken with the suspect Athens EDES, had little hesitation in publicly abjuring his connection with those who were suspected of working too closely with puppet Prime Minister Rallis and his German friends. Zervas also having agreed to remain within the area in which he had been compressed by the last ELAS attack, the only point remaining to be settled was that of forming a united guerrilla army.

As might be expected, there was a lack of agreement on the method of accomplishing this third condition.

Meeting first at Mirofillon and later at the Arakhthos River bridge at Plaka, negotiations dragged on without approaching a solution to the united army problem. Both Zervas and Psaros were unwilling to come under the direction of EAM/ELAS, while the latter, with its overwhelming numerical superiority felt, with some justice, that the united guerrilla army should be built around it. For a time it appeared that a degree of unity might be achieved by the appointing of a compromise commander-in-chief but no agreement could be reached on the man to be selected. It was even suggested by one of the delegates that the andarte forces of Greece might be brought under the command of a British general officer. To this suggestion, ELAS replied with an emphatic "No!"[26]

Politics constantly crept into the discussions but the AMM and EDES delegations refused to discuss the political aspects, maintaining that they were only empowered to act on purely military matters. However, since the basic disagreement between ELAS and EDES was ideological, it soon became clear that political differences would prevent agreement on military problems. In spite of the fact that discussions made little progress, the AMM made no effort to speed or interrupt the interminable arguments since it appeared that the longer the andarte leaders argued, the longer the truce would continue.

Although EKKA had come to the conference with a carefully neutral attitude and had readily agreed to many ELAS proposals, as time went on Colonel Psaros and his political advisor, George Kartalis, gradually swung over to support EDES. Sarafis claims that this change of heart came as a result of pressure exerted by the AMM.[27] It is more probable, however, that the EKKA delegates, warned by the intransigent attitude of ELAS, began to fear that a guerrilla army united on ELAS terms might well mark the end of EKKA.

The final result of the conference was a compromise agreement that amounted to little more than the continuation of the armistice. Signed on 29 February 1944, and known as the Plaka Armistice, the agreement contained nine points as well as a secret clause, inserted at the insistence of the AMM. The nine clauses provided for the final cessation of all hostilities between ELAS and EDES, the maintaining of positions held as of 29 January, and agreements to fight against the common enemy both jointly and individually. Also covered were methods of settling disputes between bands, release or trial of political prisoners, and an agreement for all organizations to render all possible aid to the suffering civilian populace of Greece. The secret clause was an agreement between all parties to co-operate in the implementation of Operation NOAH'S ARK, another widespread campaign of sabotage which would precede the liberation of Greece.[28]

In spite of the fact that large numbers of ELAS and EDES _andartes_ had been engaged in fighting each other for several months and that thereafter the principal _andarte_ leaders had been absorbed in truce negotiations for a considerable period, guerrilla operations against the Germans had not ceased. Under the guidance of ALO's, bands in areas removed from the disputed Epirus region had continued to harass the German lines of communication.

## German Counterguerrilla Measures

If the Germans expected that the establishment of strongpoints along the principal highways and the garrisoning of a few of the larger towns would result in eliminating the guerrilla menace, they soon discovered their error. Strongpoints and garrisons were only effective in controlling the immediately surrounding area and any objective beyond rifle range or out of sight remained a guerrilla target. The Germans found that passive defense measures were not enough and that it was necessary to conduct almost continual reconnaissance and punitive operations.

Counterguerrila operations were roughly classified into two types -- major and minor. The latter were independent punitive expeditions conducted by units of regimental size or smaller. Major operations were on a much larger scale -- planned and executed by a corps headquarters, employing at least a division -- conducted for the purpose of cleaning out large concentrations of guerrillas in an entire region.

Minor operations were usually hastily conceived as an immediate reaction to a local guerrilla attack or act of sabotage -- but were sometimes activated as a result of receiving information that a guerrilla band was present in the area. Haste was necessary in initiating such operations since the hit-and-run nature of guerrilla actions meant that delay would jeopardize any possibility of success. In most instances, the procedure was to mobilize as many troops as were immediately available and rush them to the reported location of the guerrilla band. Whenever possible, the area would be surrounded by troops who would converge toward the center in an attempt to compress and trap the band. Where conditions were favorable, machine guns, mortars, and light artillery weapons were positioned to cover the pocket formed by the converging troops. If encirclement was not feasible, troops would spread out in extended order and thoroughly comb the area as they advanced.

Occasionally, minor operations were systematically conducted by regimental-size units, utilizing the same careful planning that characterized the major operations. Such operations were normally employed to clean out a specific area in which a guerrilla band was known to be active, rather than as an immediate reprisal for an attack or act of sabotage. In spite of efforts to maintain secrecy, the preparations required were invariably observed and correctly interpreted by the guerrilla intelligence net. In addition, a regiment on the march was large enough to be detected by guerrilla outposts and yet was not sufficiently large to seal off an entire area completely. Even when most brilliantly conceived, this type of operation generally closed the jaws of the trap only to find the quarry had disappeared.

When aggressively conducted, the encirclement method was often successful in capturing or killing at least a part of the band, but combing an area in extended order was seldom effective. Intimately acquainted with every pass and goat track and not required to maintain any formation, the guerrillas would disperse and melt away in front of the slower moving conventional force. Even when surrounded, guerrilla bands were frequently successful in making an escape by slipping through even the smallest breaks in the line of encirclement.

In mopping up a guerrilla-infested area, one difficulty experienced was the reluctance of the average soldier to make a thorough check of every possible guerrilla hiding place. Knowing that capture meant death, the cornered guerrilla was a dangerous adversary. Because close investigation of every patch of brush and each rocky crevass was not only extremely dangerous but was also tedious, the troops tended to avoid the chore.

Counterguerrilla actions were not always conducted in open country. On several occasions, guerrilla bands took refuge in strategically located mountain villages and poured a murderous fire on their attackers from the protection of the stone houses. The German system for dealing with such situations was to bring up mortars and light artillery to destroy the protecting walls. If encirclement of the village could be speedily accomplished, it was sometimes possible to round up the entire defending force. In most cases, however, the German preparations were quickly analyzed by the guerrillas and the village would be evacuated before the troops or artillery could be positioned. The common guerrilla practice of widely dispersing when making a withdrawal made it difficult to conduct an effective pursuit.

The Greek andartes, particularly members of ELAS, seldom wore uniforms or distinctive insignia and it was impossible to distinguish resistance fighters from harmless civilians once the former had hidden their weapons. In the earliest counterguerrilla operations German troops permitted many guerrillas to escape, thinking they were civilians. Later, the pendulum swung the other way and the average German soldier became something less than particular about whom he shot or captured.

His reasoning was that any man found in the area was either an active guerrilla or in league with the local band. For this reason, German figures for guerrilla casualties were usually much higher than those announced by the <u>andartes</u>.

Concluding that minor counterguerrilla operations were generally ineffective, the Germans seriously considered the launching of more large-scale punitive expeditions. Major operations, however, meant the diverting of entire divisions from coastal defenses as well as requiring the consumption of fuel and other supplies that could ill be spared. After the major operations conducted to open the principal highways in the fall of 1943, no large-scale counterguerrilla operations were initiated until the late spring of 1944. Throughout December 1943 and the early part of 1944, counterguerrilla measures were restricted to the establishment of strongpoints, the conduct of minor operations, and reprisals against those who had, or were suspected of having aided the guerrilla cause.

## German Reprisals Against Civilians

As early as 16 September 1941, Field Marshal Wilhelm Keitel had issued a top secret order which branded all guerrillas as Communists and decreed that Communist hostages would be executed at the ratio of fifty to one hundred for each German killed.[30] Although this order was directed to the forces encountering Soviet partisans on the Russian front, the method of dealing with those involved in resistance movements had been established by the highest headquarters.

Hostages were sometimes taken in advance and held in prison camps where they would be handy for execution in the event of guerrilla activity in the area. Hostages were also used in an effort to deter guerrilla attacks on truck convoys and railroads -- in the lead vehicle or railroad car would be placed a number of unarmed civilians who would be the first to die in the event of an attack or the exploding of a mine.

In choosing hostages the occupation forces preferred to select community leaders and members of the Communist Party as well as those who were suspected of aiding the guerrillas. In many cases, little selectivity was exercised, the Germans merely rounded up all males, between the ages of 16 and 60, who were found in villages adjacent to the scene of an attack.

In Greece, the Germans did not, at first, employ the extreme ratio for the killing of hostages that had been recommended by Keitel. Instead, a ten-to-one ratio was put into effect. When the execution of hostages at the "mild" rate failed to deter the guerrillas, the quota was raised to the prescribed fifty-to-one.

Prosecution lawyers at the Nuernberg Military Tribunal trials of German war criminals summed up the reprisal measures in Greece in the following indictment:

> Lidice, the small Czech village which the Germans leveled to the ground in 1942, stands today as a symbol of German savagry. In Greece there are a thousand Lidices -- their names unknown and their inhabitants forgotten by a world too busy and too cynical to remember. Greece had many small primitive villages with 500 to 1,000 inhabitants who live in mud houses with thatched roofs that have been lived in for centuries. There are, for example, the villages of the Peloponnesus peninsula which were leveled to the ground in December 1943 during the notorious "Operation Kalavritha." Touched off by a report that "bandits" in the vicinity had killed 78 German prisoners, troops subordinate to

General Felmy [Lt. Gen. Helmuth Felmy, CG, LXVIII Corps] embarked on a reprisal expedition that lasted for 8 days before their senseless bestiality had been satisfied. Fourteen villages were completely destroyed and their male inhabitants shot. Five hundred and eleven persons from Kalavritha alone were executed.[31]

Counterguerrilla Measures in the Peloponnesus

In late October 1943, the 1st Panzer Division was withdrawn, leaving the 117th Light Infantry Division with the primary responsibility for the conduct of counterguerrilla operations in the Peloponnesus. Unable to adequately police its new and larger area, the division began experiencing great difficulty in controlling the guerrillas of the region. In spite of a late start, ELAS had grown rapidly in that area and, after eliminating rival ES and EOA bands, took control of large segments of the Peloponnesus. Early in December, German intelligence estimates placed the strength of ELAS forces in the Peloponnesus at three to four thousand in the southern part and five to six thousand in the north. Although these figures appear to be somewhat exaggerated, there is no doubt that EAM/ELAS had built a strong and vital organization in the southernmost part of the Greek mainland.

Since the Peloponnesus was extremely vulnerable to Allied invasion, it was important that the guerrilla menace be eliminated in order to secure German rear areas. A number of punitive expeditions initiated by the 117th Light Infantry and other units under LXVIII Corps met with little success. Failing to annihilate the guerrilla bands, the Germans turned to a safer and easier method of discouraging resistance -- reprisals against the civilian populace.

War Diary No. 3 of LXVIII Corps carries innumerable entries similar to the following extracts:

28 November 1943 -- In Old Corinth, the reinforced 117th Signal Battalion carried out a mopping up operation in the course of which 67 hostages were seized and arms and propaganda material secured.

4 December 1943 -- In Aighion, 50 hostages shot to death as a reprisal measure for attack on truck on 2 December.

5 December 1943 -- 50 hostages hanged at the railroad station of Andritsa as reprisal measure for attack on 1 December.

7 December 1943 -- 25 hostages shot to death in Gythion as reprisal measure for attack by bandits on 3 December west of Gythion.[33]

These comparatively minor reprisal actions were followed by the infamous Operation KALAVRITHA in which a total of 24 villages and 3 monasteries were destroyed and 696 Greeks, mostly civilians, were shot to death. The wholesale destruction of villages and the shooting of women and children failed to have the desired deterent effect on the guerrillas. Instead, the andartes of the Peloponnesus became increasingly active and in early 1944 a series of successful ELAS attacks required the LXVIII Corps to turn once more to operations directed solely against the guerrillas.

Operation AMSEL (Blackbird) was initiated on 13 January and, although five battalions were employed, no contact with the guerrillas had been made when the operation was concluded on 5 February. In March, a well-planned guerrilla ambush waylaid a truck convoy and 18 Germans were killed and 44 wounded. A punitive force was immediately dispatched but failed to make contact with any guerrillas. In order to insure that the efforts of the punitive force should not be totally wasted, 10 villages were razed and 200 hostages were shot. In addition, the entire

Peloponnesus was placed under martial law.

On 10 April, three counterguerrilla operations were launched simultaneously: CONDOR (Condor), REIHER (Crane), and IGEL (Hedgehog). Operation REIHER was concluded on 24 April and CONDOR on the following day; neither having succeeded in establishing contact with a guerrilla force. During Operation IGEL, the advance company of the 116th Reconnaissance Battalion was encircled by a strong guerrilla force near the town of Krokova (Dhrakovouni). In the course of the fire fight which developed, the company suffered losses of 26 dead, 30 wounded, and 61 missing. Although all other units were ordered to converge on the area of the attack, no further contact was made with the guerrillas.

The success of the guerrilla attacks and skillful evasion of the counterguerrilla forces was undoubtedly due to the leadership and tactical ability of Aris. Perhaps the most capable guerrilla leader in Greece, he had been active in forming and directing the ELAS organization in the Peloponnesus. The imposition of martial law and the harsh reprisal measures visited upon the people of the Peloponnesus did little to discourage Aris and his andartes. During the first week in May, ELAS bands ambushed and killed Major General Krech, Commanding General of the 41st Fortress Division, and three enlisted guards. In retaliation the 41st Division executed a total of 325 hostages, but an intensive search operation failed to find the andartes responsible.

The Peloponnesus was not the only area of Greece in which the guerrilla activities sparked reprisals and counterguerrilla measures. Throughout the early part of 1944, occupation forces were engaged in the conduct of counterguerrilla operations in many other regions.

## Punitive Expeditions and Massacres

In the vicinity of Salonika, a number of counterguerrilla operations were launched in early 1944. Operation WOLF (Wolf), a joint German-Bulgarian effort was begun in January and ended after 354 andartes had been killed and 400 prisoners taken. WOLF was followed shortly by Operation HORRIDO (Tally Ho) which accounted for 310 dead guerrillas and 15 prisoners. German losses in HORRIDO were 18 dead, wounded, and missing. Operation RENNTIER (Reindeer) was launched in late February and concluded in early March. The Germans claimed a total of 96 guerrillas were killed and 100 prisoners taken. There were 2 German and 7 Bulgarian casualties. A subsequent minor operation called ILTIS (Polecat) resulted in the killing of only 15 guerrillas. In the area north and west of Salonika, Operation MAIGEWITTER (May Weather) was undertaken in April. Conducted on a fairly large scale, MAIGEWITTER resulted in guerrilla losses of 339 dead and 75 captured. An additional 200 suspects were taken as hostages.

In Boeotia, northwest of Athens, Operation KULUVISTA was launched in early January and resulted in inflicting heavy casualties on ELAS bands operating in that area. In this operation the Germans learned that guerrila tactics could be profitably employed by conventional troops. Establishing an ambush, a small force surprised a company of 69 guerrillas near Koukouvista (Kaliskopi), killing them all without any losses being suffered by the attacking unit. A counterattack, launched by a strong andarte force, was contained and still further losses were inflicted on the ELAS andartes. When finally concluded,

Operation KUKUVISTA had accounted for 150 guerrillas killed, 200 wounded, and 1 prisoner. In addition, 8 machine guns and large quantities of small arms and ammunition were captured. German losses were 8 dead and 26 wounded.

Subsequent operations, such as WILDENTE (Wild Goose) which was conducted in Attica in late March, were only partially successful as the andartes employed evasive action and fled into the mountains at the approach of German troops.

The counterguerrilla measures undertaken in the regions north of the Peloponnesus were not entirely confined to military operations against armed guerrilla bands. These regions also experienced their share of burnings of towns and slaughtering of unarmed civilians. In the war crimes trials of commanders subordinate to Army Group E, the prosecution cited two major reprisal actions which serve as gruesome reminders that in guerrilla warfare the civilian populace often suffers far more than the members of the armed guerrilla bands.[34]

In April 1944, two German soldiers were killed by a guerrilla band operating near the town of Klissoura, in Thessaly. In retaliation, the 7th SS Panzer Grenadier Regiment wreaked its vengeance on the inhabitants of Klissoura. Before their afternoon's work was finished, 223 civilians had been killed -- 50 of them children under ten years of age, 128 women, and the rest old men. The younger men, thinking the women, children, and aged would be safe, had fled to the hills. The town of Klissoura was left a mass of smouldering rubble.

Minister Plenipotentiary to the Southeast Command, Hermann Neubacher, protested the wanton brutality of "The Blood Bath of Klissoura," as the Germans themselves entitled their report of the massacre. Not that Neubacher was concerned with any humanitarian considerations, his only concern was with possible political repercussions. He demanded a complete investigation and report from Field Marshal von Weichs, Commander-in-Chief, Southeast. A few weeks later Minister Neubacher received a report which was a complete whitewash of the whole affair, "The Greek witnesses cannot be believed. The village was taken by storm, the inhabitants killed by artillery fire. There was no retaliation action."

Just two months later, in June 1944, troops of the same 7th SS Panzer Grenadier Regiment repeated the Klissoura performance in the town of Dhistomon, in Attica. In retaliation for the ambushing of a company of the 7th Regiment, about a mile from Dhistomon, a total of 270 civilians were killed -- again, mostly women, children, and old men.

Minister Neubacher again protested to von Weichs, stating that the Dhistomon massacre was politically dangerous. In the course of the investigation that followed, a member of the German Secret Police testified to what he saw in Dhistomon, concluding with the statement: "As far as I could see it, all were shot dead. I did not see inhabitants being killed in any other way, i.e. beaten to death by rifle butt or by pouring gasoline over them and setting them on fire." The prosecution attorney at the Nuernberg Military Tribunals was justifiably curious to know why the secret policeman had thought it necessary to specify that he had not seen anyone beaten to death or burned alive. "Was that the usual method of executing retaliation victims?" he asked.

Commenting on the destruction of the mountain villages and the burning of food stores and crops which often accompanied such reprisal actions, John Mulgan, a British Liaison Officer says:

> Their purpose was clear in all this burning. They wanted to break the resistance movement by starving out the mountains, and also by showing the people that their andartes were worthless and offered them no protection. In a more complex civilization this might have succeeded. But the villagers, once they understood what was happening, hid their stores of grain and flocks in the hills and waited until the enemy was gone, and then moved back again into the ruins of their houses. What hatred they felt continued to be concentrated on the Germans who had burned their houses. Towards their own fighting men who had brought this on them they felt perhaps apathy and showed despair, but never hostility.[35]

The severe German countermeasures, the wholesale killing of hostages, the widespread leveling of villages, and the launching of punitive expeditions failed to halt andarte operations. Bands were frequently forced to move from districts that had been laid bare and others were forced to temporarily suspend operations, but the guerrilla movement was never snuffed out. Each new German excess only served to fan the flames of revenge and resulted in the stirring up of greater hatred for the occupation forces. The number of andartes continued to increase and ELAS, particularly, was able to build up sufficient strength to enable it to continue efforts against the Germans while simultaneously striving to wipe out all rival organizations.

## CHAPTER V

## GUERRILLA AND COUNTERGUERRILLA OPERATIONS
## (1944)

### Planning for Operation NOAH'S ARK

Following the signing of the Plaka Armistice in February 1944, conflict between EDES and ELAS ceased -- at least, temporarily. Both organizations continued to regard the other with distrust and both maintained strong forces along the joint borders of their respective territories. It was an uneasy situation which might, at any moment, again flare up into civil war. The AMM hoped, however, that anticipation and preparation for another large-scale operation against the Germans would keep the guerrilla organizations from fighting among themselves.

The secret clause appended to the Plaka Armistice had been an agreement by ELAS, EDES, and EKKA to support Operation NOAH'S ARK. Proposed by the Middle East Command, this operation was to be a campaign of widespread guerrilla violence, similar to that which paralleled the Allied invasion of Sicily. This time the Greek _andartes_ and the ALO's would have the assistance of infiltrated British commandos and American operational groups.[1] Strategically, NOAH'S ARK was conceived for the purpose of preventing a large, fully-equipped German force from withdrawing north from Greece, to insert itself between the Soviet forces advancing from the east and British-American forces moving north and east from Italy. Tactically, the operation would effect the interdiction of roads and railways in an effort to prevent withdrawing German forces from evacuating their heavy equipment from Greece. Although no specific date had been set for the implementation of the sabotage campaign, it was generally believed by the guerrilla leaders that an Allied invasion in April 1944 would cause the German withdrawal and trigger the start of Operation NOAH'S ARK. Actually, Allied strategy did not call for an invasion of Greece, but it was believed that events on other fronts would force the Germans to evacuate Greece in early 1944. Believing that the prospect of the early liberation of Greece would be another factor tending to keep the andarte organizations at peace with each other, their leaders were permitted to retain their belief in the April date.

Supply drops to ELAS which had been discontinued during the December clashes were not resumed immediately after the signing of the Plaka Armistice. Shortly after the conference, when General Sarafis asked the AMM for large-scale supply drops which would enable ELAS bands to continue current operations, he was told that the Middle East Command was not in a position to supply the 30,000 andartes which ELAS now claimed. The AMM, particularly Colonel Woodhouse, had long since come to the conclusion that ELAS was not as interested in fighting the Germans as it was in conserving its strength to support an EAM political coup after liberation. Further, it was strongly suspected that much of the material already sent in by the British had been stockpiled by ELAS instead of being expended in current operations. There was, of course, another reason for withholding large shipments of arms and ammunition from ELAS -- the AMM did not wish to furnish that organization with the means to continue its fight against EDES.

Unwilling to aid EAM/ELAS in a possible takeover of the Greek Government, and yet needing the strength of ELAS in the accomplishment of current missions, the AMM chief offered a compromise. He agreed to replace all ammunition which ELAS forces might expend in actual combat operations against the Germans. According to General Sarafis, Woodhouse also stated that all interest was now centered in the NOAH'S ARK operation and, since that operation would be limited to specific targets, it would only require the use of about 10,000 andartes, adding that the rest of ELAS should be disbanded if it could not be supported by its own facilities. In commenting on the attitude of the AMM, Sarafis said, "ELAS, which understood their purpose -- that it should find itself at the end of operations exhausted, without food, clothing or ammunition -- was now faced with a dilemma."[2] Since the close of NOAH'S ARK would, in effect, be the end of all need for a Greek resistance -- the enemy would have departed -- there was little reason why ELAS should find itself well supplied at the end of the campaign. The reaction of Sarafis was another indication that ELAS had definite plans to be implemented after the Germans had pulled out of Greece.

In spite of the fact that the British refused to give ELAS the supplies which it demanded as being absolutely necessary, that organization agreed to fulfill its obligation to support NOAH'S ARK. With this assurance, Colonel Woodhouse and his American deputy, Major Wines, set out in early March to visit various andarte areas and arrange support for the forthcoming sabotage campaign. Much to their chagrin, they were required to carry the passes which ELAS insisted that all travelers through the mountains must possess. Even though both the AMM chiefs traveled in uniform and Woodhouse was one of the best known men in Free

Greece, each local commander insisted on closely scrutinizing the bits of paper with the letters E L A S prominently displayed.

Just prior to their departure, Woodhouse and Wines were shown two disturbing documents which Zervas had taken from an ELAS courier apprehended in EDES territory.[3] Both documents had been issued by GHQ, ELAS and were addressed to all division commanders. The first directed division commanders to continue to demand arms and ammunition from the ALO's regardless of the stores they might have on hand. It added that all surplus arms should be cleaned, greased, and stored in secret depots to be saved "against the day of need." The second message advised the division commanders that Colonel Woodhouse and Major Wines would soon be passing through their territory. Commanders would advise all villages to form committees to establish contact with the AMM chiefs for the purpose of pointing out enemy damage and the villagers' economic needs -- for which immediate relief should be demanded. The first of the messages came as no great surprise as it merely confirmed already well-founded suspicions. The second, however, was a new tactic and appeared to be a typical Communist maneuver to destroy the Greek people's faith in the Allies as well as the AMM. Since the AMM was purely a military mission and had no facilities for providing economic relief for the people of Greece, the demands of the villagers would be embarrassing and the mission's inability to assist the needy people would be interpreted as callous indifference. EAM/ELAS by suggesting that the people demand assistance from AMM would be credited with having the interests of the people at heart.

During their trip the two mission chiefs saw many evidences that other copies of the messages must have gotten through. In their visits to andarte headquarters demands for arms and ammunition were always made before operational requirements or needs for equipment could be discussed. Almost every village and hamlet had its committee waiting, invariably armed with a petition -- all of which were, curiously enough, almost identical in content and phrasing.

After spending several days in talks with the military commander, capetan, and political advisor of the ELAS 9th Macedonia Division at its Pendalofon headquarters, the AMM chiefs moved on to Mavreli, headquarters of the 10th Macedonia Division. There, in early April, they received news of the formation of an EAM/ELAS sponsored government for Free Greece, the development of which had been rumored during the Plaka talks. At the same time, reports of renewed friction between ELAS and its two principal rivals were also heard. Woodhouse and Wines cut their trip short and headed back to Viniani to investigate these two most unwelcome developments.

## Provisional Government for Free Greece

On 11 March 1944, a provisional government for Free Greece was inaugurated at Viniani.[4] The Political Committee for National Liberation (Politiki Epetropi Ethnikis Apeleftherosis), or PEEA, was set up in opposition to the Government-in-Exile which EAM/ELAS had long contended was not representative. Although this contention was undoubtedly true, except in those mountain areas which EAM/ELAS had under firm control, PEEA could not lay claim to being the peoples' choice either. Established by EAM and, like EAM, theoretically nonpartisan, the provisional government was oriented well to the left. Again, like EAM, although its leadership was not predominantly Communist, by holding key positions, KKE could exercise effective control of PEEA.

Those who joined PEEA and later became disillusioned with its Communist ideology were unable to withdraw. EAM/ELAS having foreseen this possibility had published the names of all members of PEEA in the resistance newspapers of Athens. Since these papers invariably fell into the hands of the Germans the return of the deluded politicians was effectively prevented.[5]

In its formation of PEEA, EAM showed its political strength in the mountain villages of Free Greece by holding elections of village officials and members of the Bouli (parliament). Propagandized as a democratic expression of the peoples' will, the elections did not permit the voters to exercise any choice of candidates or issues as the local EAM organizations selected the candidates and ruthlessly suppressed any opposition. There was, of course, a great deal of popular support for EAM/ELAS but those who opposed its high-handed methods and brutal repressions of political opponents were often forced to seek the protection of the German-sponsored Security Battalions.[6]

It has been suggested that the villages of Greece were located high in the most inaccessible mountains in order to foil the tax collectors during the long years of Turkish occupation. However successful this subterfuge may have been in discouraging the Turks, it failed in the case of EAM. Along with the EAM version of democracy came the imposition of taxes combined with a tithing system for the support of the ELAS bands. Generally paid in kind, these taxes were undoubtedly a heavy burden on the already impoverished villagers. There is, however, no indication that the combined taxes and tithes were any heavier than those levied under the Metaxas dictatorship.[7]

## Changes in ELAS

PEEA, with its various secretariats, relieved GHQ, ELAS of many logistic and administrative chores and, as a consequence, a number of organizational changes were effected. The new provisional government provided for the dissolution of the ELAS Central Command in Athens and also eliminated the position of political advisor with the field units. In actual practice, however, the political commissars did not depart from the various headquarters -- they merely assumed military ranks and continued as staff members. To perform the military functions of the ELAS Central Command, PEEA provided a Secretary of War and for political guidance GHQ, ELAS would henceforth look to the Secretary for Home Affairs, George Siantos, former general secretary of KKE.

In addition to the changes resulting from the formation of the PEEA, other command changes were instituted in the spring of 1944 because poor communications had made it difficult for GHQ, ELAS to maintain control over distant units. In an effort to overcome this weakness, greater autonomy was given to regional commands. The northern divisions were grouped under a corps headquarters known as the Macedonian Group of Divisions. The 9th and 10th Macedonia Divisions were assigned to the new corps headquarters and instructions were issued to form a third division -- the 11th. Within a few weeks, similar corps headquarters were established in Thessaly and Attica.

The new command changes moved ELAS still further along the road in its efforts to achieve conventional status. The GHQ, ELAS directive of 1 September 1943, redesignating its units as divisions, regiments, and battalions, had been a first step in the attempt to conventionalize. ELAS' subsequent acquisition of large quantities of Italian equipment and heavy weapons had also been instrumental in moving the andarte organization in the same direction. This trend toward conventionality was largely due to the efforts of General Sarafis and the many former army officers who had, by early 1944, joined ELAS. His first observations of guerrilla tactics had failed to impress Sarafis and he recorded his disapproval of units which failed to stand and fight. Later, in discussing the Battle of Porta, he noted with pride that, for the first time, a guerrilla force had conducted a static defense, "This action showed the Italians that they no longer had to do with guerrillas but with disciplined troops who knew how to fight, . . ."[8]

The pride of a professional soldier in seeing a well-organized army develop from a motley collection of untrained, unco-ordinated bands is understandable. ELAS, however, was better organized on paper than on the ground and as it gained in conventional organization, it lost its effectiveness for the only type of fighting it was equipped to do. It was deficient in many things necessary to a conventional force: communications, transport, heavy weapons, training, and individual discipline. Conventional in command structure only, it ceased to be a guerrilla movement without achieving the efficiency of a well-integrated military force.

With the exception of the major headquarters, most of the andartes were still organized as 20- or 30-man bands which were only assembled to form larger forces on rare occasions. In many cases these small bands did little but garrison villages which did not require garrisons or guarded passes through which the Germans never had, or never would, come.[9]

A British soldier who escaped from a German prison in Greece took shelter with a guerrilla band which, he claimed, lived partly by stealing, partly by "sponging on" relatives in nearby villages: "They were an idle, drunken crowd and we spent most of our time in the cafes. While in their company I was very seldom sober."[10]

Without orders from a higher headquarters the ELAS <u>andartes</u> seldom engaged in the hit-and-run raids which had characterized their tactics in the early days of the movement. Small, local raids were, apparently, beneath the dignity of the army, corps, and division headquarters which ELAS had built up. Plans and preparations were now made for large-scale operations which meant that the element of surprise -- so vital to guerrilla actions -- was lost. Required to organize in large groups for attacks on well-defended installations, the assembling of the <u>andartes</u> was invariably detected by German intelligence agencies. Although field units forwarded reports of operational successes to ELAS headquarters, the planned operations were seldom successful and, in many cases were not even attempted.

In commenting on the guerrilla forces of 1944, one of the British Liaison Officers who worked closely with ELAS units in Thessaly during 1943 and 1944 says:

Somehow, it seemed to me, the movement had outgrown itself and become militarily worthless. At some stage, Greek army officers, whose sense of dignity and grandeur outweighed their intelligence, had made a movement which should have been small, compact and irregular in design, into a vast army. They spoke now of divisions, regiments, battalions, first, second and third bureaux. With this went all the trappings and organization of regular warfare but they lacked, of course, those things that are necessary to regular war, like a system of supply, proper arms, and a uniform, tested corps of officers and men. They had nothing but contempt for the small, personally led bands with which the movement had started. Their new army gave them a sense of dignity and status; the fact that it was of no military value didn't strike them.[11]

Overorganization did not mean, however, that the guerrilla movement was dead or that ELAS was completely ineffectual. Where aggressive leadership existed and in districts where communist influence was weak, individual bands continued to interdict and harass enemy communications and supply lines. Working with, and sometimes leading those bands which still retained a degree of independence the ALO's, which numbered close to 400 by the middle of 1944, kept up a continual campaign of sabotage.[12] Many of their operations were inconsequential, but taken altogether they compiled an impressive total of destruction of railroads and other installations vital to the Germans.

The Greek Army Mutiny

Regardless of the opinions on the effectiveness of the EAM/ELAS fighting forces, there was never any doubt concerning the efficiency of the EAM propaganda machine.[13] In addition to winning Allied-world support for ELAS as the only real fighting force of the resistance, EAM propaganda was largely responsible for fomenting dissension in the ranks of the Greek Army in Egypt. On 1 April 1944, in a protest against the monarchist Government-in-Exile, large numbers of the men in the Greek Army and Navy mutinied. By 22 April, the mutiny had been quelled and

British forces had disarmed the Greek Army while loyal Greek personnel had regained possession of ships held by the mutineers.

Because of the unstable position of the Greek Government as opposed to the power of EAM/ELAS, no widespread reprisals or executions followed the mutinies. As soon as the Greek Army had been disarmed, the soldiers were given an opportunity to make a simple choice. Those who agreed with the mutineers were marched off to detention camps, while those who declared for the present government were formed into a new unit -- the 3d Brigade. The 1st and 2d Brigades ceased to exist. The division split the Greek Army almost precisely in half, ten thousand choosing detention and an equal number remaining loyal.[14]

In subsequent action in Italy, the 3d Brigade distinguished itself by taking the town of Rimini and was, thereafter, popularly referred to as the Rimini Brigade. The Sacred Squadron, a unit composed entirely of former Greek officers, had not participated in the revolt and also remained in being. In the two units which remained as the Greek Army, sentiment was strongly anti-Communist, if not strongly monarchist. Later, their presence in Athens became one of the principal causes of dissension between EAM and conservative members of the Greek Governement.

Further Territorial Disputes

Because the boundary question had not been definitely settled by the Plaka Armistice, no lines had been drawn to demark all EKKA, EDES, and ELAS territorial limitations. During the armistice discussions it had been agreed that a joint commission would meet for the purpose of formally delimiting operational areas and zones of influence. In March and April, before the joint commission could convene, several boundary disputes arose between EKKA and ELAS. Both organizations claimed that the other was violating both letter and spirt of the armistice and relations deteriorated badly. After a number of minor armed clashes had occurred, an effort was made by General Sarafis to effect a temporary compromise but no mutually acceptable decision could be reached. On 17 April, at the direction of PEEA, ELAS mounted an all-out attack against EKKA. Colonel Psaros was killed and his force completely dispersed -- many of its members escaping across the Gulf of Corinth to join the Security Battalions on the Peloponnesus. General Sarafis expressed himself as being grieved to hear of the death of his old friend of many years' standing.[15]

A few days after the annihilation of EKKA, General Zervas and his EDES force began a territorial expansion which resulted in clashes with ELAS. In this case the AMM was successful in securing a cease-fire and in bringing EDES and ELAS representatives together at Koutsaina (Stournareika) for the long-delayed conference to complete the work of the Plaka Armistice. Despite the efforts of the AMM, it appeared that no settlement would be reached and it was feared that the minor clashes might again expand into full-scale civil war. Eventually, after much persuasion, Zervas agreed to halt his expansion moves and ELAS was restrained by a desire not to jeoparize delicate political negotiations which were in progress.

Government of National Unity

The conciliatory attitude displayed by ELAS at Koutsaina was occasioned by the fact that representatives of PEEA, EAM, and ELAS were en route to a meeting with the Government-in-Exile. It was hoped that discussions would result in forming a government that would be truly representative and universally acceptable. Held in Beirut, the meeting resulted in the signing of the Lebanon Charter which established a "Government of National Unity," with a coalition ministry which included EAM personnel.[16] Although a majority of the delegates attended with a sincere desire to co-operate, it appears obvious that the die-hard KKE core in Greece had no intentions of having their delegates do anything other than torpedo the conference. After the charter had been signed and all parties had agreed to accept fair representation in the new government, EAM repudiated the whole thing before its delegates returned to Greece.[17]

## EDES Again Expands

On or about 19 June, Zervas again attempted to clear ELAS out of his area, this time moving to the south to attack the ELAS 24th Regiment near Preveza. He justified his action on the dual grounds that ELAS was occupying EDES' Epirus territory and that he needed the farm produce in that area to maintain his food supply. In a matter of days the 24th Regiment had been decisively defeated and, on 3 July, EDES attacked German forces to seize a ten-kilometer stretch of coastline in the vicinity of Parga. Holding his newly won territory against a number of minor counterattacks, Zervas established a port of entry through which were landed strong reinforcements from Italy, both British and Greek. The augmented EDES force soon had a strength of approximately

10,000 and again represented a real threat to both the Germans and ELAS.

Determined to settle with EDES once and for all GHQ, ELAS directed the massing of a force of five or six divisions, including the 9th and 10th from Macedonia. Before troop deployments could be made, German forces launched a major counterguerrilla operation in Macedonia, surrounding the ELAS 9th Division and threatening to destroy it. The attack on EDES was postponed.

Operation STEINADLER (Stone Eagle)[19]

Between 6 and 14 June, the German XXII Mountain Corps, using the 1st Mountain Division, Division Group Steyrer, and a provisional division composed of special guard battalions with Greek, Polish, Russian, and Ukranian personnel, had conducted Operation GEMSBOCK (Mountain Goat). Deploying in the mountains of southern Albania, the three divisions had been successful in compressing the guerrillas into a small area near the sea, killing or capturing between 2,000 and 2,500 Albanian guerrillas. Losses of the German forces were 120 killed and 300 wounded.

Inspired by the success of GEMSBOCK, a similar plan was implemented to destroy Greek guerrilla forces in northwestern Macedonia. Operation STEINADLER, also conducted under the direction of the XXII Mountain Corps, employed the 1st Mountain Division, a provisional division from the Salonika Corps Group, and a number of special guard battalions. Air reconnaissance and intelligence information had indicated that the ELAS 9th Macedonian Division had its headquarters in Pendalofon and that there were some six to eight thousand guerrillas in the surrounding Pindus and Grammos Mountains.[20]

Preparations for STEINADLER were made in utmost secrecy. A minimum of staff officers and commanders were told of the plan and the troops were led to believe that they were to engage in a series of minor operations. In addition, troop movements and simulated combat preparations were made in other parts of the country to divert attention from the Macedonia area. Radio silence was observed regarding troop movements into the area and planes which conducted reconnaissance continued on beyond western Macedonia to fly over other sectors as well.

The XXII Mountain Corps planned to encircle an area, roughly oval in shape, extending about 60 miles from Ioannina north to Kastoria and some 35 miles from Grevena west to Konitsa. Four assault forces, each of approximately regimental strength, converging from strategic points around the perimeter of the oval, would drive the guerrillas toward the center, compressing them within an ever-narrowing pocket. To close possible escape routes through the rugged Grammos Mountains into Albania, a force of special guard battalions would be emplaced in a series of strongpoints. This static blocking force was positioned along the northwestern rim of the oval, on a line following the road from Leskovic northeast through Erseke and Shtike to Korca, just inside the Albanian border.

By 3 July, assembly of three of the four assault forces was complete and the blocking forces were in position along the Leskovic-Korca road. The Southern Assault Force, formed from the 1st Mountain Division, was deployed along a line extending from Malakasi, just west of Metsovon, to Ioannina. The Western Assault Force, also composed of 1st Mountain Division units, assembled in the area between Ioannina and Leskovic. The Northern Assault Force, formed from the Salonika provisional division,

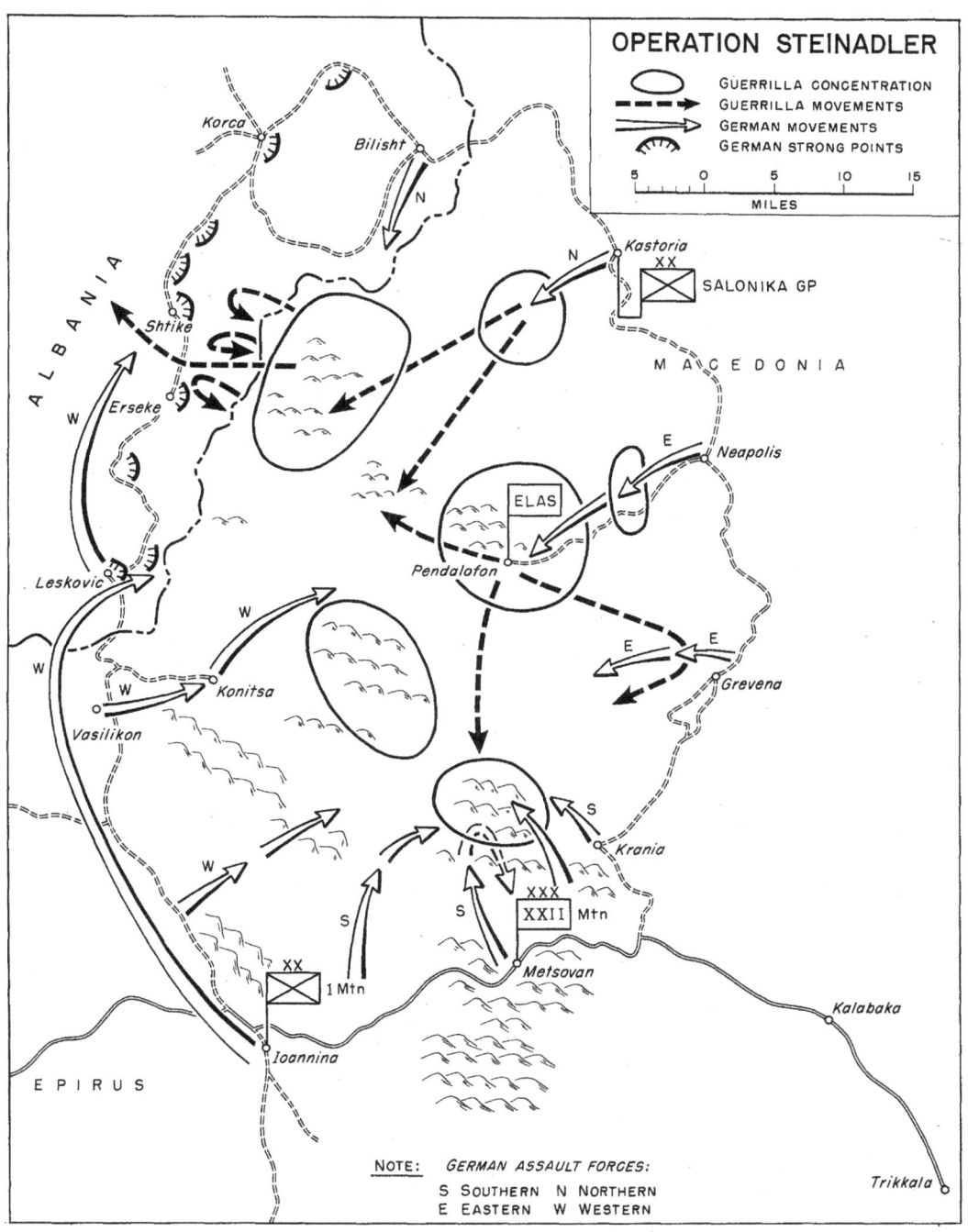

Map No. 3

was in position north of Kastoria and Bilisht. Assembly of the Eastern Assault Force, also formed from the provisional division, had been delayed, but would be completed in the area northeast of Grevena the following day.

In spite of the elaborate precautions taken to preserve secrecy, some security leaks apparently developed, as the guerrillas were not taken completely by surprise. Air reconnaissance reported that evacuation of the Pendalofon headquarters began simultaneously with the arrival of the first assault forces at their assembly areas.

On 4 July, the Northern Force, which had jumped off late the previous day, met with strong resistance from guerrilla forces occupying well-prepared positions. In a series of sharp attacks, the Germans overran the guerrilla defenses and continued to advance southward, against determined rear-guard holding actions conducted by the withdrawing guerrillas. The Eastern Force, having completed its assembly, began its advance and reached the line Neapolis-Grevena-Krania in time to thwart an attempted guerrilla breakthrough in the vicinity of Grevena. Reconnaissance detachments of the Southern Force were brought to a halt by strong guerrilla forces in the vicinity of Mount Avgo. The Western Force proceeded in a northwesterly direction without making guerrilla contact. During the night of the 4th, the blocking force reported guerrilla probing attacks and reconnaissance activity in the vicinity of Erseke and Shtike. Fearing a breakthrough, the 1st Mountain Division sent reinforcements to bolster the strongpoints in that area.

Advances by the Western, Northern, and Eastern Forces continued during 5 July, while the Southern Force was held in the Mount Avgo region by the strong guerrilla concentration which had halted the advance elements of the force. Spirited rear-guard defense actions continued to slow the advance of the Northern Force and also resulted in some elements of the Eastern Force losing contact with their headquarters and flank units.

By 6 July, the northern arc of the encirclement was completed when the Northern Force made contact with flank units of both the Eastern and Western Forces. During the 7th, the three forces continued to move toward the center, still further compressing the guerrillas and pushing them to the south. Several guerrilla supply depots, containing weapons and ammunition, were captured but only negligible losses were inflicted on the guerrillas. The Southern Force, still unable to advance, made preparations for a co-ordinated attack. The 1st Division units sent to reinforce the strongpoints, arrived too late to prevent a large guerrilla force from escaping through a gap in the line between Erseke and Shtike. It was believed, however, that the main strength of the ELAS 9th Division was still contained within the pocket being developed by the four assault forces.

On 8 and 9 July, the advancing assault forces continued to drive the guerrillas farther south, but encountered only sporadic resistance. About 120 guerrillas were killed and a number of prisoners were taken in a series of local actions. An attack launched by the Southern Force failed to crack the guerrilla defenses in the Mount Avgo region but the unit advanced when the right wing of the Western Force rendered an assist by attacking the guerrilla right flank.

Meanwhile, there was activity in the area to the south and west, where EDES forces had closed the road from Ioannina to Arta. Troops of the 1st Mountain Division were diverted to reopen the road and fought several sharp skirmishes with small EDES bands along the Ioannina-Igumenitsa road. In aggressive actions on 9 and 10 July Zervas' units were cleared from the vicinity of the main highways and large quantities of ammunition and other supplies were captured.

Throughout the 10th, small-scale battles in the operational area north of Metsovon and Ioannina resulted in 102 guerrillas being killed and 56 prisoners, inclduing 2 British, being taken. The advancing assault forces also destroyed or captured considerable quantities of small arms and ammunition. The circle around the 9th Division was tightened on the 11th and all German advances were temporarily halted in order to comb rear areas for bypassed guerrilla units.

During the last two days of the operation, the four assault forces attacked the encircled guerrillas but found only about 1,500 had been trapped. The Germans assumed that the number of guerrillas that had escaped into Albania on the night of the 7th had been considerably larger than had been estimated at first.

Operation STEINADLER was concluded on 14 July. Subsequent tabulations indicated that guerrilla personnel losses had totaled 455 confirmed dead, with an additional 400 to 500 being estimated as killed or wounded. A total of 976 guerrillas, 341 Italians, and 7 British were captured. A large number of weapons, including 519 rifles and 48 machine guns had fallen into German hands, together with 376,000 rounds of small arms ammunition, 4,000 artillery shells, and 1,000 grenades of various types. In addition, over 10 tons of mines, dynamite, and other explosives were either captured or destroyed. Some 19 large and small ammunition, clothing, and ration depots were destroyed and several thousand head of sheep and goats were taken.

In an attempt to divert German attention from their northern Greece operations, ELAS mounted a series of diversionary attacks in the southern Pindus Mountains, while Aris carried out extensive operations in the Peloponnesus. Although moderately successful in themselves, there is no indication that these diversionary attacks shortened or otherwise affected Operation STEINADLER. They did, however, cause the Germans to plan another large-scale operation in the Agrinion-Karpenision area.

Throughout the period of the attack on the 9th Division, General Sarafis had repeatedly called on the AMM to furnish additional ammunition, claiming that supplies on hand were inadequate. Although not conclusive evidence, the German figures for captured war material would tend to lend substance to the AMM contention that ELAS was stockpiling rather than expending their ammunition and explosives. While the quantities of captured material would not be large amounts for a conventional force to possess, by guerrilla standards the ELAS 9th Macedonian Division had been extremely well supplied when the German struck.

## Soviet Liaison Mission

On 28 July, shortly after the conclusion of Operation STEINADLER, a group of Soviet Liaison officers were landed at the Neraidha airstrip and proceeded to GHQ, ELAS. Sarafis and other EAM/ELAS leaders were delighted with this sign of USSR recognition and confidently expected to be the recipients of massive Soviet military aid. Although the Soviet officers listened to ELAS' pleas and agreed to submit a request for support, they made no commitments and offered no encouragement.

Like so many Soviet and Communist maneuvers, the purpose of the Soviet visit remained obscure, but it is probable that it was chiefly to obtain first-hand information on the Greek guerrilla movement.[21] It is, however, interesting to note that within a month after the arrival of the Soviets, PEEA adopted a radically different line. Not only did the provisional government agree to support the Government of National Unity but it also agreed to send representatives to participate as ministers.[22] While the new EAM/ELAS conciliatory spirit may have been due to instructions from the Soviet mission, it is possible that it resulted from a realization that there would be no Soviet military support and that EAM/ELAS must continue to look to the Middle East Command for all assistance.[23] ELAS leaders were unable to understand the Soviet mission's apparent lack of interest, but Woodhouse explains it by saying that the guerrilla leaders tried to impress the Russians with their headquarters organization but failed to show them any fighting.[24] At that time, the Soviet Union was primarily interested in winning the war and co-operation with the British was paramount. It is probable that the USSR did not desire to support EAM/ELAS in opposition to the desires of its ally.

Operation KREUZOTTER (Viper)

In the attempt to relieve pressure on the ELAS 9th Macedonian Division during Operation STEINADLER, several ELAS attacks had been initiated against supply lines, strongpoints, and seaports within the sector of the 104th Light Infantry Division, south of Epirus. In addition, Zervas' EDES force had again become active and had continued to hold its coastal beachhead in the vicinity of Parga. The presence of strong ELAS forces south of Epirus suggested that they, too, were contemplating the seizure of a strip of coast south of the Bay of Arta. With the arrival of the ELAS 7th Brigade and intelligence reports indicating that other guerrilla forces were en route to the area, Army Group E determined to take immediate and drastic action to eliminate the guerrilla menace in Epirus and Roumeli.

Operation KREUZOTTER was planned as a joint effort of the XXII Mountain and the LXVIII Corps, to be conducted in three phases. Driving simultaneously from east and west, task forces would converge on Karpenision, in the north-central part of Roumeli, with the objective of trapping a large part of the four to six thousand guerrillas estimated to be in the area. Following the destruction of ELAS forces in that region, the task forces would move into the second phase to eliminate ELAS concentrations in Boeotia, east of the Pindus Mountains. The final phase of the operation would be directed against Zervas, whom the Germans hitherto regarded as a part-time, although not entirely reliable, ally.

Operation KREUZOTTER opened on 5 August, as two forces from the west, designated Task Forces Ludwiger and Doerner, drove northeast from Agrinion heading in the direction of Karpenision. Simultaneously, Task Force Schlaetel moved westward from Lamia, also moving toward Karpenision. Intensive searches of areas parallel to the lines of march were made by all task forces as they advanced. A number of vil-

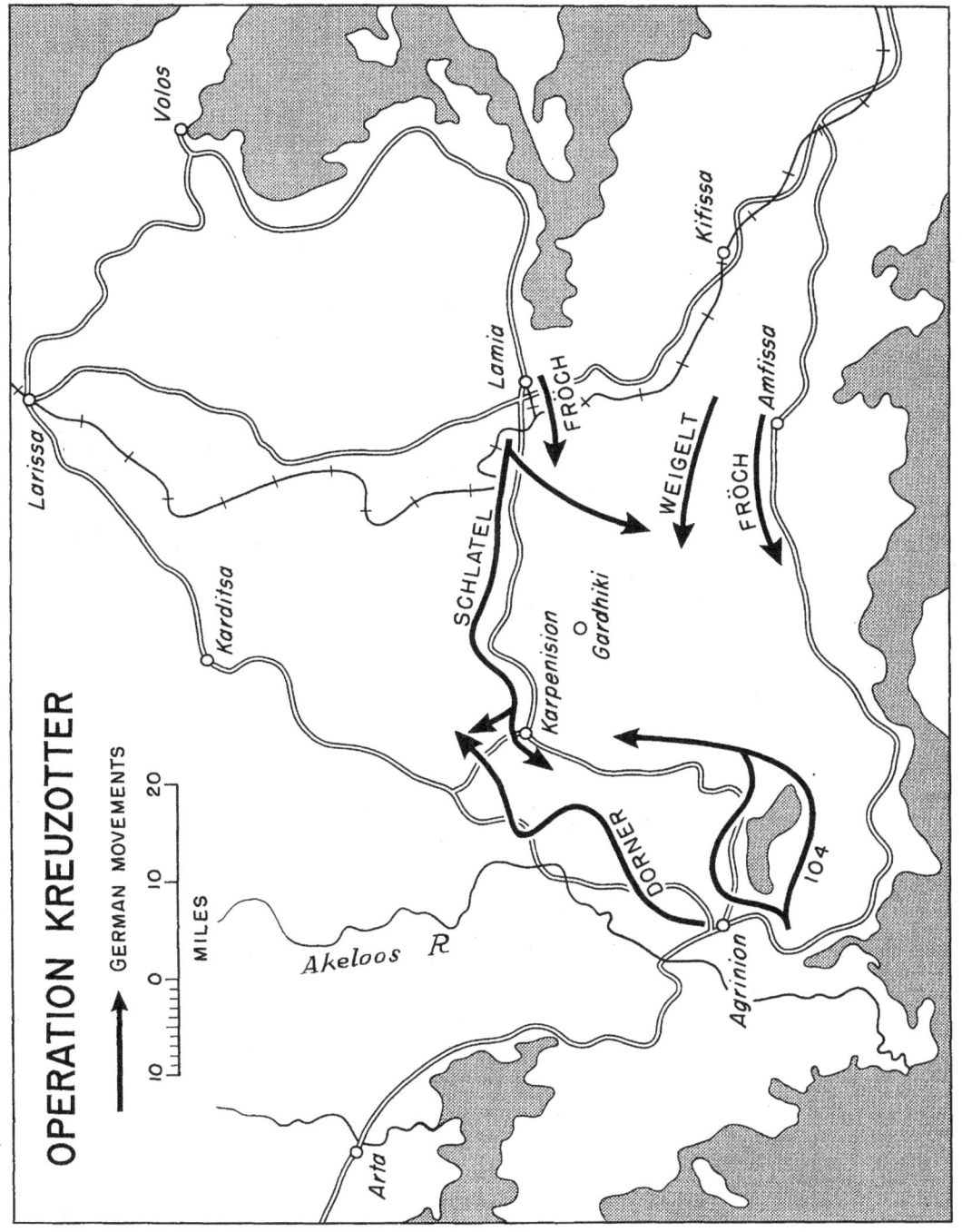

Map No. 4

lages which were suspected of harboring or supplying andarte bands were destroyed.

On 6 August, possibly as a diversionary action, a strong ELAS force attacked elements of the 3d Battalion, 18th Police Regiment, engaged in reconnaissance west of Amfissa. The 1st Battalion was immediately dispatched to the aid of the hard-pressed reconnaissance unit. After a number of sharp clashes, the ELAS force was driven off on 7 August, but the 3d Battalion had been badly mauled, sustaining several hundred casualties. Sarafis, harping on his favorite theme, says that ELAS forces would have inflicted greater losses had the andartes not run out of ammunition.[26]

In spite of encountering strong resistance, Task Force Schlaetel reached Karpenision on the 10th. Continuing to advance north and east, a link-up with Task Force Doerner was effected on the 11th. On 12 August, it was decided that, since the guerrillas had scattered throughout the mountains and no large concentrations had been trapped, task forces would conduct intensive mopping-up operations in the Roumeli region. At the same time, in retaliation for the attack on the 18th Police Regiment unit, a special task force was directed to carry out reprisals in the area west of Amfissa.

By 15 August, the initial phase of KREUZOTTER was considered completed. The western task forces, which had swung down from Karpenision in pursuit of ELAS units, continued to conduct patrol and mop-up activity without much success. KREUZOTTER II, the second phase of the operation, was initiated by the eastern task forces under direction of the LXVIII Corps. Task Force Schlaetel was withdrawn to the area between Karpenision and Lamia where, strongly reinforced, it made a number of probing attacks to the south. Task Force Weigelt, starting from a point south of Lamia, moved northwest in the direction of the Schlaetel Force. Still farther to the south, Task Force Froech conducted reprisal operations to the west and northwest of Amfissa, burning villages and crops.

On 20 August, the official conclusion of KREUZOTTER was announced and on the following day, KREUZOTTER II was also concluded. The first two phases of the operation had been only partially successful, although large quantities of weapons, ammunition, and demolitions were captured or destroyed, only 298 guerrillas were killed and 260 captured. German losses totaled 20 dead and 112 wounded, exclusive of the heavy losses suffered by the 18th Police Regiment at Amfissa. In addition, the Roumeli area was only briefly cleared of guerrillas, as ELAS units began a re-entry into Karpenision as soon as the German troops were withdrawn.

When Operation KREUZOTTER began, the XXII Corps had not yet definitely determined the precise course of action to be taken against Zervas and his EDES force in the third phase of the operation. Two alternatives had been suggested: one, that EDES be completely destroyed; the other, that efforts be made to eliminate British influence and then pressure Zervas into co-operating in actions against ELAS. Prior to the conclusion of KREUZOTTER, XXII Corps requested permission from Army Group E to conduct the operation against EDES. Immediate objectives would be limited to the capture of Paramithia and the seizure of the Parga beachhead. A decision on future actions would be made after a clear picture of EDES' strength and dispositions had been obtained. Actually, neither destruction of EDES or elimination of British influence was accomplished. Although a number of minor local engagements were fought, particularly in the Ioannina-Igumenitsa area, no large-scale operation was initiated against EDES. By 21 August when Operation KREUZOTTER was concluded, more important considerations had diverted German attention from Zervas and his bands.

### EAM/ELAS Change of Heart

In early August, General Sarafis visited Macedonia in an attempt to assess the situation of the 9th Division after Operation STEINADLER. In the midst of his tour he was recalled to the south by the news of Operation KREUZOTTER. Arriving in the vicinity of Karpenision on 21 August, he found the operation -- which he described as one of the largest scale battles fought by ELAS -- virtually concluded.[27] Following a regrouping of forces, GHQ, ELAS again began making plans to move against Zervas.

Meanwhile, Brigadier Benfield, commanding SOE Cairo, had arrived in the mountains of Greece. The purpose of his visit was to assess the current situation personally and attempt to resolve the differences between ELAS and EDES. His visit having created a temporary feeling of goodwill between the AMM and ELAS, the guerrilla headquarters had hopes that supply drops might be resumed. Under such circumstances it did not appear to be an appropriate time to start operations against EDES. In addition, there had been a change in party line and PEEA had now decided to support the Government of National Unity established at the Lebanon Conference. Again the attack on Zervas was postponed.

# CHAPTER VI

## LIBERATION AND POLITICS

### Operation NOAH'S ARK

By the end of August 1944, it had been determined that Army Group E would withdraw all forces from southern Greece to establish a line across the northern part of the peninsula -- from Igumenitsa, through Ioannina and Metsovon, to the Mount Olympus region.[1] Outlying units were pulled in and concentrated in the larger towns and cities, prepared for the northward movement.

As the time for the implementation of Operation NOAH'S ARK drew near, elements of the British Raiding Support Regiment (RSR) and a number of American Operational Groups (OG's), under the direction of the U.S. Office of Strategic Services, were infiltrated into Greece. Some came by air, but the majority were brought in by sea, either through the EDES beachhead on the west coast or via the Aegean Islands from whence they were smuggled to the east coast in Greek fishing boats. In this latter operation ELAN, the naval arm of EAM/ELAS was responsible for transporting some 300 RSR and OG personnel.[2] Operating in conjunction with the ALO's, the trained RSR and OG saboteurs raised the destruction potential of the Allied forces in Greece to a new high.

The OG's, some 12 teams scattered throughout Greece, had a strength of 24 men and 2 officers for each team. All were volunteers and many were of Greek birth or parentage. In the disruption of the railways, which was their principal task, the OG's customarily disabled locomotives with one or two well-placed bazooka shells, tore up the armored guard cars with additional rounds, and then sprayed the coaches with machine gun fire.[3]

On or about 10 September, the Middle East Command released orders for the initiation of NOAH'S ARK -- the withdrawal of the German forces was imminent. ALO's, British commandos of the RSR, American OG's, and a comparatively few guerrillas went into action. Highway and railroad bridges were destroyed, mined roadblocks were set up, trains carrying German troops and equipment were attacked or derailed, and communications were disrupted.

In Epirus, EDES engaged forces of the XXII Mountain Corps and the latter was hard-pressed to keep the Ioannina-Arta road open to withdraw its units from southwest Greece.[4] Severe losses suffered by EDES in these engagements may have been partially responsible for the inability of that organization to withstand subsequent ELAS attacks.[5] In the north, Anton Tsaous and his bands, supported by Bulgarian units, harassed and hindered German troop movements and were denounced by EAM/ELAS for collaborating with the Bulgarians.[6] ELAS, conserving its forces for other purposes did little to hinder or speed the departure of the enemy.[7] For the most part, the ALO's and commando units operating in central Greece received their only guerrilla support from independent bands which the British and Americans were able to inspire or coerce into assisting them in sabotage operations.[8] Along the eastern coast of Greece the main efforts of the saboteurs were directed at the disrupting of the Athens-Salonika railroad on which the German LXVIII Corps was barely able to maintain traffic.

Much credit, perhaps a major portion, for German personnel and material losses is due the RAF and the U.S. Air Force which conducted a number of massive air raids as well as strafing troop trains and convoys.[9]

## The Caserta Agreement

On 15 September, with the NOAH'S ARK sabotage campaign just getting under way, Generals Zervas and Sarafis were summoned to Mediterranean Theater headquarters in Caserta, Italy. There they met with General Sir Henry Maitland Wilson and members of the Greek Government of National Unity which had recently moved from Egypt to Italy. After several days of conferences and discussions, in which the EAM/ELAS representatives showed a most conciliatory spirit, an agreement was signed on 26 September.[10]

Under the terms of the Caserta Agreement the Greek guerrilla organizations acknowledged the authority of the Government of National Unity headed by Papandreou. In turn, the Papandreou government placed all guerrilla forces under the command of Lieutenant General Ronald McK. Scobie. EDES and ELAS agreed to co-ordinate their actions against the enemy and gave assurances that neither would attempt to seize the reins of government after liberation. The Security Battalions were denounced as enemy formations -- to be dealt with when their German sponsors had departed. To maintain law and order during the period between German evacuation and the assumption of control by the Greek Government, the country was divided into zones of responsibility. Each zone was specifically assigned to one of the guerrilla forces -- along the general lines established by the Plaka Agreement -- two exceptions being the Athens-Attica and Salonika-Thrace regions which were to be under direct control of the Greek Government. Having signed the agreement, Zervas and Sarafis returned to Greece to direct their respective forces in support of NOAH'S ARK.

British and Greek Army forces to be sent to Greece under the command of General Scobie were designated as Force 140, while RSR units and others already in the country were established as Force 133. Troop units assigned to Force 140 were the British 2d Parachute Brigade, 23d Armored Brigade, the latter reorganized as an infantry unit, elements of the Raiding Support Regiment, and the Greek Sacred Squadron. Upon his arrival in Greece, General Scobie would take command of Force 133, as well as Greek police and gendarmerie.

Operation MANNA, the move which would place Allied forces in temporary control of Greece, was designed primarily to prevent a take-over of governmental power by EAM/ELAS.[11] General Scobie's tasks were only incidentally connected with the withdrawing Germans, as no large-scale engagements of British vs. Germans were contemplated. Scobie was charged principally with the responsibility for maintenance of law and order, the bringing in and distribution of relief supplies, and facilitating the establishment of the regularly constituted Greek Government. Brigadier General Percy L. Sadler, U.S. Army, was appointed Deputy Commander in charge of relief and rehabilitation.[12]

## The German Exodus

By the middle of September it had become obvious to the German High Command that Russian advances in southwestern Europe would soon sever German lines of communication through Jugoslavia and Bulgaria. In October, the order was given for the complete evacuation of Greece.

During the first days of September, the German command in Greece had made efforts to evacuate the surrounding islands but both plane and ship movements were virtually brought to a halt by Allied control of sea and air. A few of the smaller islands were successfully evacuated but it was not possible to remove the garrisons from the major islands of Crete and Rhodes.

The British plan for Operation MANNA called for Force 140 to move directly to the Greek mainland, while the Greek Sacred Squadron and British commando units would occupy the smaller islands as they were evacuated by the enemy. It was decided that the island strongholds of Crete and Rhodes would be bypassed and cut off to wither away rather than incur the heavy casualties which would undoubtedly result from any attempt to dislodge the strong German garrisons.

The middle of September saw the southern part of the Peloponnesus abandoned by the Germans and, on 16 September, British commando units landed on the island of Kithera, just off the southernmost point of the Greek peninsula. Possession of this strategic location permitted harassment of any attempt to remove the German garrison from Crete and facilitated subsequent landings in the Peloponnesus. On the 23d, British units, which included an RAF regiment (less planes), were brought in to repair the air base at Araxos, in the northwestern part of the

Peoloponnesus. Within a few days, detachments had advanced to Patras which was surrendered by local Security Battalions. Brigadier G. M. Davy, in command of operations in the Patras area, made immediate contact with Aris and was able to exercise some control over ELAS and prevent <u>andarte</u> reprisals against the Security Battalions.

In early October, commando units landed at Nauplion, on the east coast of the Peloponnesus, and subsequently moved north to Corinth, accepting the surrender of Security Battalions at both locations. On 12 October, elements of the 4th Parachute Battalion and the 2d Parachute Squadron were dropped at Megara Airfield from whence they moved to nearby Athens. On the following day, commando units and elements of the Sacred Squadron landed at the port city of Piraeus and proceeded to take over the Kalamaki Airfield. By 16 October, General Scobie was in Athens to be followed on the 18th by Papandreou and principal Greek governmental officials.

Although General Scobie sent one paratroop brigade northward to keep the retreating enemy moving, little damage was inflicted on the Germans as they were moving too fast for effective pursuit action. The British advance was slowed by supply and communications problems as well as the many celebrations which joyful Greeks along the route insisted on holding. The pursuit was also delayed by the fact that there were almost no highway bridges -- sabotage which had been well advanced by Force 133 had been completed by the Germans. As a consequence, the pursuing British forces were frequently more than a day behind the German rear guard.[15]

Results of NOAH'S ARK

Despite promises to attack and harass the retreating Germans, ELAS actually did little damage to the departing enemy.[16] The leaders of EAM/ELAS were saving their strength for other purposes. Some made an attempt to justify their inactivity by pointing out very logically that the Germans were pulling out of Greece as quickly as possible -- "Why do anything that might delay this much desired evacuation?" On the other hand, it was obvious that EAM/ELAS recognized an obligation to make some attempt to destroy the Germans' future military potential. The leftist press made exaggerated claims of tremendous victories and strove to convince the Greek people as well as the outside world that ELAS was taking a bloody and terrible revenge against the oppressors of Greece.

Near Kozani, near the Jugoslav border, in a battle between the retreating German forces and a small British unit, ELAS <u>andartes</u> were present but took no part other than remaining in a position to protect the flanks of the British force. In some sharp fighting, the British lost fourteen killed and a number wounded while guerrilla losses were nil. The following day, the Germans evacuated the town and ELAS forces entered hard on the heels of the German defenders. Within a matter of hours, <u>Eleftheria</u> the Macedonian EAM news-sheet carried the following story:

Severe fighting took place on the 26th and 27th of October on the heights above Kozani where our units shattered enemy resistance and captured Prophitis Ilias, which commands the town. In this battle our andartes fought with unparalleled heroism and determination. After the battle for the heights the attack began on the town itself. After a bitter five-hour fight Kozani was taken and the enemy is now in retreat northwards towards Amyntaion. Enemy losses in the battle were huge and rich booty was captured. The extent of both has still to be fully calculated.[17]

Other greatly magnified figures indicating tremendous losses inflicted on the retreating Germans were published throughout Greece, particularly in the leftist press. In spite of the unreliability of the sources these inflated figures were generally believed -- probably because ELAS did possess the capability of inflicting such casualties. Claiming a strength of 50,000, if ELAS had applied itself to the task in hand as enthusiastically as its press proclaimed, Army Group E might well have been eliminated as an effective fighting force.

The Greeks were not the only ones to be misled by the Communist propaganda, the American press and at least one eminent British historian were also deceived.[18] Official German casualty figures, however, fail to substantiate the guerrilla claims. While losses were heavy, they were considerably less than the leftist press indicated. From 10 September, the start of NOAH'S ARK, to 31 October, when the last German units were leaving Greece, Army Group E suffered the following casualties: Killed, 1,450; wounded (and presumably evacuated), 5,422; missing, 997.[19] It should be borne in mind that, during this period, troops of Army Group E were moving northward into Bulgaria and Jugoslavia and meeting strong opposition there. Therefore, not all of the announced German casualties can be assumed to have occurred in Greece.

Maintenance of Public Order

The fine spirit of andarte co-operation displayed at Caserta disappeared in the mountains of Greece. Speeding the departure of the enemy was too often forgotten as both EDES and ELAS were occupied in wreaking bloody revenge on political opponents and the taking over of some disputed territories was frequently accompanied by clashes of arms between the two guerrilla groups. Generals Zervas and Sarafis personally did their best to carry out the terms of the Caserta Agreement, but were unable to control the actions of hotheads and fanatics of both sides.[20] The rift between EDES and ELAS was too wide to be closed simply by the affixing of signatures to a paper and no real degree of unity or co-operation was achieved.

In spite of excesses committed by the lunatic fringe of the guerrilla organizations, law and order in the liberated areas was maintained reasonably well. Only in Macedonia was there widespread fighting between Greeks as ELAS moved against independent bands and some rather large groups of collaborators which had long been present in the northern area. Anton Tsaous and his Greek Nationalist Guerrilla Bands were accused by ELAS of collaborating with the Bulgarians and fighting against, rather than amalgamating with ELAS. The fact that the Bulgarians had, early in September, come over to the Allied side and had agreed to fight the Germans, was ignored by ELAS. For much of the trouble experienced with Anton Tsaous, ELAS blamed the ALO assigned to that area, claiming that the latter was supplying Anton's bands with arms and ammunition which were being used against ELAS. In this, ELAS was probably partially correct -- there is little doubt that Anton Tsaous did fight ELAS, but he also did what ELAS frequently failed to do, he fought the Germans.[21]

By the end of October, the ELAS Macedonian Group of Divisions had most of Macedonia under its control; the collaborationist bands had been broken up, the Bulgarians had left Greek soil, and only Anton Tsaous remained. By 4 November, the last of the Germans had retreated across the northern borders of Greece. With the exception of Athens, which was under the control of the Greek Government; most of Epirus, which still remained as EDES domain; and Anton Tsaous' small part of Macedonia, ELAS was in complete control of Greece.

## Political Maneuvering in Athens

The Germans had evacutated Athens on 12 October and the rejoicing city had lain wide open to ELAS had EAM desired to take over the government. The small British force which entered Athens hard on the heels of the withdrawing Germans could not have prevented a determined effort by EAM/ELAS. Had the <u>andarte</u> organization seized their opportunity, ELAS could only have been dislodged by force of British arms, a maneuver which Allied public opinion might well have prevented.[22] ELAS had the forces available for an Athens take-over, even as the Germans moved northward strong ELAS units had been moving to the south, converging on Athens. That EAM did not take advantage of so obvious an opportunity is probably attributable to the fact that the proponents of peaceful infiltration held the upper hand at the moment.[23] The people of Greece and even EAM/ELAS joined in welcoming the British forces and for a short time it appeared that all would go smoothly in the transition period. Although there was some skirmishing between ELAS and X, in Athens, it was on a small scale and did not appear to pose a serious problem.[24]

EAM had not, however, given up its intentions of taking over control of the Greek Government. The peaceful interlude that followed liberation merely indicated that there was disagreement as to the method to be employed -- peaceful infiltration or seizure by force. Athens was full of ELAS Reservists and the city was virtually surrounded by ELAS field units of the 1st Athens Army Corps which checked all movement in and out of the city. In effect, the Papandreou Government was held prisoner in Athens by EAM/ELAS.[25]

While EAM politicians engaged in political squabbling, ELAS voiced complaints about the treatment it was receiving. It claimed it had saved the country and that its divisions represented the armed forces of Greece. In their self-proclaimed roles as the heroes of the resistance, its leaders resented being ignored by General Scobie and Papandreou. Among the principal complaints were that ELAS had received no orders or directives from the War Minister, that its forces had been required to hold up at the northern borders of Greece and had not been permitted by General Scobie to pursue the Germans into Jugoslavia, that no provision was being made for supply or hospitalization of ELAS andartes, and that ELAS had not been permitted to have at least one of its divisions enter Athens for a victory parade. The minor annoyances built up to major disagreements and differences were magnified out of all proportion to their importance. From a joint victory celebration with mutual feelings of British-Greek good-will, the situation deteriorated to a point where there were frequent incidents between individual British soldiers and Greeks. In some areas there were serious clashes between ELAS and British troop units. General Sarafis described the British attitude as unreasonable and claimed that General Scobie had wrongly accused ELAS of using terrorism to disrupt relations between the Greek people and the British. According to the ELAS commander's account, he was warned that this practice would cease and that the situation would show an immediate improvement or the British would take the necessary steps to insure proper respect.[26] Although General Sarafis is inclined to twist facts to suit his own ends and is not invariably the most reliable of sources, there is no doubt that General Scobie did threaten to use force if ELAS attacked British soldiers.[27]

As the situation deteriorated, the British realized that the token force of approximately 10,000 would not be sufficient to maintain control should ELAS attempt to take over by armed force. Additional divisions were brought in bringing the total British strength in November to 22,600 troops and 5 air squadrons with additional divisions en route or held in readiness in Italy.[28]

The Demobilization Controversy[29]

In the final analysis, it was the question of demobilization that brought about an open break between EAM/ELAS and the British. On 22 November, Papandreou announced that all volunteer military forces would be disbanded. To replace them a National Guard would be formed by calling up pre-war Reserve classes. Papandreou's subsequent attempts to obtain the full agreement of his coalition government resulted in the development of tremendous opposition from the EAM members. The principal point of contention was over the status of the 3d Greek (Rimini) Brigade which had been brought to Athens from Italy on 10 November. When Papandreou let it be known that he contemplated using the brigade as a nucleus for the new National Guard, EAM violently opposed him, claiming that it was a royalist force/which would be used to re-impose the monarchy. Although the brigade was definitely anti-Communist and probably pro-monarchist, it is doubtful if that single brigade, even with British support, could have effected the return of King George II -- there was too much popular opposition. EAM members of the government also presented a strong argument in holding that the 3d Brigade was a volunteer unit, just as was ELAS, and that a general demobilization of volunteer forces should include it as well as the guerrilla forces.

General Scobie, apparently becoming impatient with the endless political squabbling, determined to take matters into his own hands. On 26 November, he conferred with Generals Zervas and Sarafis, presenting his plan for the demobilization of ELAS and EDES. He explained that Papandreou's concept of a National Guard would be followed and that a force of 35 battalions each with 30 officers and 600 men would be formed. He added that the Reserve class of 1936 was already being called up and would be used to replace the gendarmerie which were to be screened to eliminate those who had been collaborators. All andartes, including both ELAS and EDES, would be disarmed and released during the period between 10 and 20 December. Zervas agreed to the proposal but Sarafis raised numerous objections.

The ELAS commander claimed, with some accuracy, that General Scobie was exceeding his authority. Under the terms of the Caserta Agreement, ELAS had agreed to come under the operational direction of the British general, but the demobilization of the Greek Armed Forces was not operational -- it was a matter which should be reserved to the Greek Government. Sarafis intimated that the British were interfering too much in matters that were purely internal Greek affairs and demanded a government decree directing demobilization of the guerrilla forces. He also took exception to the disarming of the andartes, stating that the men should be allowed to take their weapons home as symbols of their fight against oppression. In addition, he wished assurance that ELAS officers would have rights of reinstatement and promotion in the National Guard. The meeting ended without agreement.

Meanwhile Lambrianidhis, Assistant Secretary of War, had been forced to resign when EAM proved that he had commissioned and enlisted large numbers of former Security Battalion personnel in the National Guard. EAM also claimed that reserves were being called up only from areas of known royalist sympathies. Lambrianidhis was replaced by Saryiannos, an EAM nominee, appointed in an attempt to mollify that organization. To EAM/ELAS, this attempt to load the National Guard with men opposed to Communist ideology was a final, convincing argument that the government was trying to force the return of the monarchy.

On 27 November, it appeared that a compromise between EAM and conservative members of the government had been reached. The 3d Brigade plus an EDES unit of undetermined size together with an ELAS force, equal in numbers to the two other units, would be integrated under a single command. By 29 November, however, the EAM members of the government had changed their minds and refused to concur in the compromise to which they had already given tacit approval. They again insisted that the 3d Brigade be demobilized.[30] It would appear that they had been informed by those with broader military experience that an ELAS force equal in numbers to the 3d Brigade would not be its equal in armament, training, or fighting ability. Now completely fed up with political vacillation and wrangling, General Scobie directed that demobilization take place on 10 December as originally announced.

During the period since liberation, the proponents of direct action within EAM had, through propaganda and persuasion, been able to win over the advocates of peaceful infiltration. By the end of November, plans for a forceful takeover of the Greek Government were well under way. The ELAS Central Command which had been abolished in March had been reconstituted with General Mandakas, former PEEA Secretary of War, and George Siantos in control.[31] GHQ, ELAS was notified by the EAM Central Committee that again it had come under the direction of the ELAS Central Command. A directive to the ELAS headquarters ordered it to place the 1st Athens Army Corps, the Central Greece Group of Divisions (2d and 13th), the 3d Peloponnesian Division, and the Cavalry Brigade under the direct control of the Central Command. The designated units were ordered to move to Thebes (Thivai), just north of Athens. All other ELAS units remained under command of GHQ, ELAS.

On 2 December, in a protest against the demobilization order and in an attempt to hamstring the government, the six EAM ministers in the Papandreou Cabinet resigned en bloc. Simultaneously, EAM requested and was granted permission to hold a political demonstration in Constitution Square on Sunday the 3d. Later the same day a general strike was announced for Monday, the 4th, and the ELAS Reserves of Athens and Piraeus were called up. Getting wind of the massive preparations for the demonstration and apprehensive of EAM's intentions, the British persuaded Papandreou to withdraw permission for the demonstration. It was too late. The EAM plans were too far advanced to be cancelled -- even if its leaders had wanted to do so.[32]

## Disorders in Athens

The general strike started prematurely and all utilities in Athens ceased to function on Sunday as demonstrators began flocking into the center of the city. The small Athens police force had been ordered to prevent demonstrators entering Constitution Square and had thrown cordons across the streets leading to it. Most of the police were armed with Italian carbines which were, theoretically, loaded with blank ammunition. A few, however, must have slipped live rounds into their weapons when they noted that many of the demonstrators were armed. When a crowd began to push through one of the cordons and force its way into the square, the police panicked and opened fire. Several demonstrators fell to the ground. Although EAM later claimed that all police fired live ammunition, this contention is disproved by the fact that only about seven marchers were killed and an equal number wounded -- had all the police fired live rounds into the densely packed crowd, the number of casualties would have been much greater.

As news of the shooting spread throughout Athens, a frenzy swept the thousands of demonstrators and crowds attacked police stations, beating and killing a large number of police. A crowd estimated at fifty to sixty thousand milled about in Constitution Square for the better part of the day -- dipping their banners into the blood of the dead and wounded while swearing vengeance on the fascist spillers of innocent Greek blood. British troops were finally called out to succor the beleagured police force and, in the evening, a company of British soldiers cleared the square without difficulty.

On the following day, 4 December, the bodies of the slain marchers were paraded through the streets of Athens, but there was little disorder during the march. The British had been warned and, as a result, tanks and armored cars lined the parade route. Later in the day, a group of ELAS Reservists attacked the headquarters of X, and its defenders were only saved from extinction by the arrival of a strong British force. That night General Scobie ordered all ELAS units to vacate Athens immediately.

On 6 December, EAM/ELAS attempted to take over all government buildings to effect a political coup. Again the British had been warned, the buildings were all guarded by British troops and the attempt failed. Although a few shots were exchanged, ELAS forces were still reluctant to attack the British.

At that time, Scobie's forces in Athens were quite small, consisting of a brigade of paratroopers, an armored brigade, and the 3d Greek Brigade, totaling about 6,000 combat troops with an additional 4,000 service personnel. ELAS, on the other hand, had nearly 15,000 Reservists in Athens and approximately 8,000 andartes from Thessaly were en route or in the Athens suburbs. In addition, a force of 2,000 men from the 3d Division had been brought up from the Peloponnesus by Aris and was moving on Piraeus.

Following the unsuccessful attempt of EAM/ELAS to take over the government buildings, the British launched an air attack on Ardettos Hill, to the south of Athens, where a large ELAS force had assembled. A follow-up infantry assault, launched by the 3d Brigade, was repulsed and the brigade was subjected to heavy sniper fire from the Kaiseriani district in southeast Athens. On 10 December, a small British force occupied the Army Cadet College to the north of the city, but the detachment was promptly besieged by a strong ELAS group. The garrison was relieved the next day, but only after several tanks and armored cars had been wrecked by ELAS mines.

Civil War in Athens[35]

The situation in Athens became increasingly serious but, until 12 December, ELAS still hoped that the British would not interfere in the quarrel between EAM and the Papandreou Government. This was, of course, wishful thinking as the British forces were definitely committed to the support of the established government of Greece. In an effort to persuade the British to remain neutral, George Siantos had a number of conferences with General Scobie. They solved nothing. The general still stuck to his previous ultimatums that ELAS must get out of Athens, disband, and turn in all weapons.

Meanwhile, between 8 and 12 December, in defiance of General Scobie's orders, ELAS continued to move units into positions in the Athens area and to compress the British forces. A few British troops were isolated on the tip of Piraeus and a slightly larger unit held Hassani Air Base and a strip of shoreline along the Gulf of Phaleron. The main British force was boxed into a small sector of Athens -- an area five or six blocks wide and less than two miles in length. British detachments, located throughout Greece, were pulled back to the larger cities: Athens, Volos, Salonika, and Patras. Supplies of food and ammunition were extremely short and the British position in Athens was so desperate that General Scobie seriously considered evacuating the city.

On the night of 15 December, ELAS launched an all-out attack on the small British sector in central Athens. Fortunately for General Scobie's small force, the attack was poorly co-ordinated and armored units were able to rush from one trouble spot to another and repulse the attacks. Fortunately for the badly outnumbered British, few of ELAS' efforts were fully co-ordinated. In addition, the Communists spent much time in acts of vengeance -- killing hostages and launching continued attacks on Averof Prison in an attempt to capture or kill Rallis and Tsolakoglou, prime ministers under the occupation, as well as other collaborators imprisoned there.

On 18 December, ELAS struck at the RAF headquarters at Kafissia, a suburb of Athens. After a two-day fight, the headquarters was overrun and the guerrillas took several hundred prisoners. This was the high point for ELAS in the battle of Athens -- from that date on the fortunes of the guerrillas declined. Conversely, the British situation showed rapid improvement as additional supplies and a steady stream of both Greek and British reinforcements poured in.

The Greek Government had called up Reserve classes for the years 1934 through 1940 and the National Guard was speedily built up -- perhaps too speedily. With most of Greece in control of ELAS, the only source of National Guard recruits was from a comparatively small part of Athens. Desperate for manpower, little attention was paid to the characters of those enlisted. As a consequence, a large number of hoodlums as well as collaborators from the Security Battalions were accepted. These first National Guard units which later came to be known as the "Athens Battalions" were of low caliber and had a bad reputation throughout Greece. In addition, the gendarmerie which had been sent to Athens for the purpose of being screened to eliminate collaborationist elements, was enlisted en masse without any background checks being made. Later, greater care was taken in accepting enlistments, but under the pressure of the ELAS attacks there was no time to be selective. By the end of December, the National Guard had been built to thirty-six battalions with 19,000 men armed and equipped.

Two British divisions were withdrawn from the Italian front and rushed to Greece together with an Indian brigade and several miscellaneous battalions. With this strength on hand by late December, the British were prepared to launch a counteroffensive, but delayed for political reasons.

### ELAS Operations Outside Athens[36]

Not all of ELAS was involved in the battle for Athens. As the ELAS Central Command and the 1st Athens Army Corps made preparations for action in the capital, other important tasks were assigned to GHQ, ELAS.

At the same time that it had directed the dispatch of ELAS divisions toward Athens, the Central Command had also ordered GHQ, ELAS to eliminate the forces of Zervas and Anton Tsaous. Later, after the fighting had broken out in Athens and British units throughout Greece had been withdrawn to a few cities, ELAS was also given the task of maintaining surveillance over the British garrisons. Although Sarafis expressed his willingness to attack and disarm the British, the Central

Command asked only that they be kept bottled up and under observation. The watch on the city of Volos paid ELAS handsome dividends. When the British evacuated the city on 16 December, they abandoned much equipment which ELAS promptly appropriated as spoils of war. The 104 trucks and large quantities of food and fuel which the <u>andartes</u> gained were of tremendous assistance in reinforcing and supplying Athens.

The 6th, 10th, and 11th Divisions of the Macedonian Group had disposed of Anton Tsaous by 12 December and GHQ, ELAS was able to send a part of that force south to Athens. In addition, units were sent to join the forces surrounding the British in Salonika, while others went north as frontier security detachments. Meanwhile, the 1st, 8th, and 9th Divisions were converging on Epirus for the attack on EDES.

Under the personal direction of General Sarafis and the redoubtable Aris, the campaign against Zervas was launched on 21 December. The 8th Division, attacking from the south, succeeded in taking Arta within a day. The 1st Division, coming from Larisa via Metsovon, cooperated with the 9th Division, moving down from Albania, to capture Ioannina on the 23d. Thereafter the 9th Division drove west to take the port city of Igumenitsa, while the 1st Division joined the 8th to attack Zervas' last stronghold at Prevesa. By 29 December, the operation was concluded, EDES had been defeated with amazing ease. Those EDES <u>andartes</u> which were not scattered were evacuated to Corfu by the British Navy.

General Sarafis claims that the ELAS force employed in the attack on EDES totaled 11,500 and that Zervas had 9,000 men. While his figure for ELAS' strength may be accurate, his estimate for EDES appears to be somewhat high. Heavy losses suffered just prior to and during the German evacuation had reduced Zervas' force to approximately 8,000, according to XXII Mountain Corps' estimates.[37]

The British were unable to account for Zervas' poor showing in the fight against ELAS. As attested by both British and German observers, EDES was by far the better trained and equipped of the two guerrilla organizations and in a defensive situation Zervas should have been capable of containing an attack by vastly superior forces. In extenuation, Woodhouse points out that Zervas was a victim of his own integrity; that he had started demobilization in accordance with General Scobie's instructions; that he had been required by the British to turn over large quantities of small arms ammunition to ELAS (during NOAH'S ARK) which then fired it back at him; and that Zervas did not have the heart to engage in a conflict that pitted Greek against Greek.[38] While these arguments are undoubtedly true, it is hard to believe that the wily Zervas should suddenly become so naive as to completely demobilize in the face of the very obvious ELAS threat. As far as his reluctance to pit Greek against Greek, Zervas had never before hesitated to fight ELAS when it suited his purposes. It appears that some other, more conclusive reasons must be sought to account for his failure to fight the fight that had been expected of him.

It is probable that, the country having been liberated, many of Zervas' men decided to go home and that some voluntary demobilization had taken place. Unlike ELAS, EDES had no plan to retain a large fighting force after the Germans had departed. There is also a strong possibility that ELAS had succeeded in subverting many EDES men who wanted to be on what, at that time, looked like a winning side. The New York

Times, for December 26, 1944, quotes its correspondent as saying that many EDES were deserting to ELAS and that Zervas' force had been reduced from 12,000 to a total of between 4,000 and 6,000 due to casualties, desertions, and turncoating.

By inference, it is possible to suggest another explanation for Zervas' hasty withdrawal in the face of the ELAS attack. Somewhere between 5,000 and 7,000 EDES andartes and an equal number of supporters were evacuated by the British Navy -- a fairly large operation. To divert that much naval support to Zervas at a time when such forces were badly needed elsewhere would indicate that the EDES evacuation was directed by a higher headquarters than that of Force 140. It is quite possible that the move was set up by Mediterranean Theater headquarters or even the British Prime Minister, who was in Athens at the time. With the British hard-pressed in Athens and under pressure in Patras and Salonika, the Mediterranean Command might well have considered that several thousand EDES andartes might better be preserved as a reserve rather than wasted in defending strategically unimportant Epirus.

There is, of course, another possibility. When ELAS first attacked, Zervas had called on the British for assistance but, with their resources already strained to the utmost, no aid could be sent. Realizing that full-scale war with ELAS would be costly and convinced that the British would defeat ELAS anyway, Zervas may have decided that he had nothing to gain from such a fight. When the British offered to evacuate his force he may, in true guerrilla fashion, have made the decision to fight and run away and thereby live to fight another day.

Immediately after the conclusion of the successful operation against EDES, Sarafis received word that the situation in Athens had deteriorated seriously. On 2 January, Aris sped to the capital to render what assistance he could while General Sarafis remained behind to supervise the dispatch of the 9th Division and one regiment of the 1st Division as Athens reinforcements.

## Peacemaking Efforts[40]

On Christmas Day of 1944 Winston Churchill had flown to Athens in an attempt to effect a political compromise that would put an end to the fighting by establishing an acceptable and stable government. In a series of conferences, conducted under a flag of truce, EAM representatives remained adamant and refused to make any concessions, while rightist elements, confident of full British support, were equally intransigent.

Convinced that EAM and KKE would have to be completely crushed before they would accept what the British considered reasonable terms, Mr. Churchill directed the strongly reinforced British forces to launch a full-scale offensive against ELAS.

Meanwhile the discussions dragged on while the British waited impatiently for the Greeks to arrive at some workable solution to their problems. The only point on which a measure of agreement could be reached was that a regent should be appointed to serve as the head of the Greek Government until a plebiscite should determine the form of government desired by the people. On every other issue EAM and the conservative group were hopelessly at odds and unable or unwilling to give ground. Even the British Prime Minister, experienced in the diversities of politics, lost patience with the interminable bickering and arguing of the Greek politicians. On 28 December, after making a few rather undiplomatic, but highly descriptive, remarks regarding Greek politics, Mr. Churchill took off for England.[41]

In London, the British Prime Minister called on King George of Greece and prevailed on him to permit the appointment of a regent. Word of the king's assent was immediately flashed to Athens and, on 1 January 1945, Archbishop Damaskinos was installed as regent. General Nicholas Plastiras, returned from his exile in France, accepted the post of prime minister. This change of regime met with general approval throughout Greece and was responsible for winning many of the more moderate members of EAM away from the influence of the communist elements.

The British Offensive[42]

Early in December, command of the British forces engaged in the Athens fighting had been given to General Hawkesworth in order to relieve General Scobie of the burden of directing combat operations.[43] In addition, General Hawkesworth's broad field experience was considered to be preferable to General Scobie's staff background in a combat situation. General Scobie, however, retained his position as commander of all British and Greek military forces in Athens as well as other parts of Greece.

Losing no time in carrying out Prime Minister Churchill's orders, General Hawkesworth began his offensive on 27 December. It soon became evident that ELAS had underestimated the capabilities of the British troops or had not been aware of how strongly they had been reinforced. Pressing north from his base on the Gulf of Phaleron, General Hawkesworth had little difficulty in driving back the ELAS forces. The 3d Greek Brigade broke through the encirclement of their barracks and advanced south toward the center of Athens. Within three days the southern half of the city and most of Piraeus had been cleared of ELAS forces. The new National Guard battalions saw little action in the combat operations, being used almost exclusively in guard duty and in rounding up the many snipers that harassed the British advance.

Pausing in Athens for a few days, General Hawkesworth regrouped his forces and, on 3 January, resumed his attack. Although they fought more determinedly than they ever had against the Germans, the ELAS forces were no match for the stronger and better equipped British.[44] By 4 January it was obvious to the ELAS Central Command that it could no longer hold any part of Athens and a general withdrawal was ordered. The pull-out was conducted in good order with rear guard actions as well as destruction of roads and bridges holding up the British pursuit. By 6 January, all ELAS field units had cleared the city, taking with them some 15,000 hostages in retaliation for rumored cruel treatment of ELAS prisoners by the British and Greek Army units. For the most part, the ELAS Reserves hid their weapons and returned to their homes.

After mopping up in and around Athens, on 8 January the British advance was continued -- moving, during the following week, northwest to Lamia and south to Corinth. The battle of Athens was over and the back of EAM/ELAS was broken. In spite of the fact that there were still many thousands of ELAS <u>andartes</u> in other parts of Greece, EAM realized that it had failed in its bid for power. In addition to being defeated, the attack on their British allies combined with acts of terrorism had cost EAM/ELAS most of its popular support.

On 11 January, delegates from the ELAS Central Command approached General Scobie to arrange an armistice. Within two days an armistice and cease-fire agreement was concluded. Terms of the armistice required ELAS to evacuate the southeastern part of central Greece, including the districts of Attica, Boeotia, and a portion of Phocia as well as the area in a 20-mile radius of Salonika. All ELAS units were to be returned to their home territories and all prisoners and hostages were to be released. Hostilities would cease on 15 January, pending a permanent peace settlement.

In the fighting in and around Athens, British casualties had totaled 27 officers and 93 enlisted men killed, 202 officers and 988 enlisted men wounded, and 16 men missing.[45] The number of Greek hostages who died of exposure and starvation or were brutally murdered will probably never be known -- estimates place such deaths as high as 5,000.

## The Varkiza Agreement[46]

Although it had been dealt a severe blow, ELAS did not disband or disintegrate after the signing of the armistice. With no assurance that a permanent peace settlement would be effected, ELAS began a regrouping of forces, preparing to return to the mountains and a renewal of guerrilla warfare. It was still a force to be reckoned with and was well supplied -- the stockpiles accumulated prior to liberation having been augmented by captured German, British, and EDES equipment.

While peace negotiations were still pending, EAM tried to utilize the potential strength of ELAS to improve its bargaining position at the conference table. EAM/ELAS insisted on sending noncommunist delegates to the peace conference while the government and General Scobie were equally insistent on dealing with communist members as representing the controlling faction of EAM/ELAS. Eventually, the Greek Government and the British prevailed and, in early February, George Siantos and two other Communists came to Athens to begin the negotiations.

The wrangling and bickering so typical of negotiations with Communists continued for several days and it was not until the 12th of February that an agreement was reached. Taking its name from the small town in which the final signing took place, the treaty became known as the Varkiza Agreement.[47] Under its terms, ELAS would surrender all arms and would effect complete demobilization within two weeks. In return, the government decreed amnesty for all political crimes committed during the period from 2 December until the date of the signing of the agreement. Provision was also made for the upholding of civil liberties and for the punishment of collaborators. A National Army was to be formed by calling up appropriate classes of reservists, but it was specified that professional soldiers would be retained -- in effect, keeping the controversial 3d Brigade and the Sacred Squadron in service. Finally, a general plebiscite would be held to determine the future form of the Greek Government.

Within the specified time, rather to the surprise of the British, ELAS carried out the demobilization and disarming of its forces. There were, quite naturally, a number of violations and many die-hards, including Aris, refused to surrender their arms or be demobilized and fled to the Pindus Mountains vowing to continue the fight for their particular version of democracy.

By 28 February 1945, ELAS had ceased to exist and the Greek resistance movement of World War II had ended.

CHAPTER I

1. Athens and its port city of Piraeus are normally considered as constituting a single metropolitan area.

2. For an exposition of the plotting and interminable discussions of Athens politicians and military leaders, see: Stefano Sarafis, *Greek Resistance Army* (London: Birch Books, 1947), pp. 1 - 6.

3. Unless otherwise specified, material used in the following two sections has been taken primarily from C. M. Woodhouse, *Apple of Discord* (London: Hutchinson & Co., 1948); William Hardy McNeill, *The Greek Dilemma: War and Aftermath* (Philadelphia and New York: J. B. Lippincott Co., 1947); and Sarafis, *Greek Resistance Army*.

4. "Few people knew or even guessed, until the Germans left in 1944, that the EAM was Communist dominated." Chris Jecchinis, *Beyond Olympus* (London: George W. Harrap & Co., Ltd., 1960 ), p. 28.

5. Resistance organizations will be discussed in greater detail on pages 17 to 24 below.

6. Hugh Seton-Watson, *The East European Revolution* (London: Methuen & Co., Ltd., 1950), p. 133.

7. Material used in the following two sections has been taken primarily from Woodhouse, *Apple of Discord*; McNeill, *The Greek Dilemma*; and L. S. Stavrianos, *Greece: American Dilemma and Opportunity* (Chicago:

Henry Regnery Co., 1952), hereafter referred to as Stavrianos, <u>Greece</u>.

8. William Hardy McNeill suggests that the name ELAS was chosen because of its phonetic similarity to ELLAS, the Greeks' name for their country. (<u>The Greek Dilemma</u>, p. 75.)

9. L. S. Stavrianos, "The Greek National Liberation Front," <u>Journal of Modern History</u>, No. 24 (March 1950), pp. 42 - 55.

10. Woodhouse, <u>Apple of Discord</u>, p. 63.

11. According to C. M. Woodhouse, the word <u>Dhimocraitikos</u> may be translated as Democratic but, in domestic politics, is understood to mean <u>Republican</u>. (<u>Apple of Discord</u>, p. 73.)

12. Richard Capell, <u>Simiomata, A Greek Note Book</u> (London: Macdonald & Co., Ltd., 1946), p. 79.

13. <u>Tsaous</u> was the Greek interpretation of the Turkish word for <u>sergeant</u>. Hence, the pseudonym adopted by this guerrilla leader meant <u>Anton the Sergeant</u>. His real name is variously reported as Anton or Andon Filiates and Andonius Fosteridhis.

14. The role and activities of the British Military Mission will be more fully discussed in later portions of this book.

15. Unless otherwise noted, material on Sarafis is taken from Sarafis, <u>Greek Resistance Army</u>.

16. E. C. W. Myers, <u>Greek Entanglement</u> (London: Rupert Hart-Davis, 1955), p. 148.

17. McNeill, *The Greek Dilemma*, p. 77.

18. Myers, *Greek Entanglement*, p. 114.

19. The assumed name of this Communist leader is spelled both as *Aris* and *Ares* by writers of the Greek guerrilla movement. William Hardy McNeill suggests that the name *Ares* was selected as a classical allusion to the Greek god of war. (*The Greek Dilemma*, p. 63.)

20. Woodhouse, *Apple of Discord*, p. 65.

21. Gerald K. Wines, Major, USA (Ret), A Lesson in Greek, unpublished MS, 1948, pp. 33 - 34.

22. Denys Hamson, *We Fell Among Greeks* (London: Jonathan Cape, 1947), p. 98.

23. McNeill, *The Greek Dilemma*, p. 64.

24. Hamson, *We Fell Among Greeks*, pp. 95 - 97; Myers, *Greek Entanglement*, p. 69.

25. Woodhouse, *Apple of Discord*, pp. 77 - 81.

26. *Ibid.*, p. 73.

27. McNeill, *The Greek Dilemma*, p. 65.

28. Stavrianos, *Greece*, p. 67; Woodhouse, *Apple of Discord*, p. 80.

29. Myers, *Greek Entanglement*, p. 220.

30. Sarafis, *Greek Resistance Army*, p. 60.

31. Woodhouse, *Apple of Discord*, p. 85.

32. See p. 19 above.

33. McNeill, *The Greek Dilemma*, p. 76.

34. Chandler, *The Divided Land*, pp. 16 - 17.

35. Sarafis, *Greek Resistance Army*, p. 127.

36. General Hubart Lanz, Partisan Warfare in the Balkans, MS # P-055a, OCMH files, p. 31.

37. Constantinos Trianaphylidis, testimony August 16, 1947 before the American Military Tribunal, Nuernberg, Germany. (U.S.A. vs Wilhelm List, *et al*., case No. 7, vol. 7, mimeographed records), pp. 2102 - 3.

38. Lanz, Partisan Warfare in the Balkans, pp. 62 - 64.

39. Chandler, *The Divided Land*, p. 15.

40. Lanz, Partisan Warfare in the Balkans, pp. 36 - 38.

41. Wines, A Lesson in Greek, p. 172.

42. Testimony of Constantinos Triandaphylidis at the American Military Tribunals, August 16, 1947, pp. 2087 - 89.

43. McNeill, *The Greek Dilemma*, pp. 75 - 76.

44. *Ibid*., pp. 80 - 81.

45. Testimony of Constantinos Triandaphylidis at the American Military Tribunals, August 16, 1947, p. 2113.

46. Myers, Greek Entanglement, p. 120.

47. McNeill, The Greek Dilemma, pp. 61 - 62; Hamson, We Fell Among Greeks, pp. 104, 119.

48. Lanz, Partisan Warfare in the Balkans, pp. 24 - 26.

49. Testimony of Constaninos Trianadyphlidis at the American Military Tribunal, 16 August 1947, pp. 2099 - 2100; Lanz, Partisan Warfare in the Balkans, pp. 26 - 27.

50. W. Stanley Moss, A War of Shadows (New York: The Macmilan Co., 1952), p. 72.

51. M. B. McGlynn, Special Service in Greece (Wellington, N.Z.: Pamphlet published by War History Branch, Department of Internal Affairs, 1953), p. 8n.

52. Woodhouse, Apple of Discord, p. 66. Testimony of Constantinos Triandaphylidis, American Military Tribunal, 16 August 1947, pp. 2119 - 21.

53. Myers, Greek Entanglement, p. 73.

54. Wines, A Lesson in Greek, p. 73.

55. Ibid., p. 168.

56. Sarafis, Greek Resistance Army, p. 310.

57. Stavrianos, Greece, pp. 70 - 71.

58. Hamson, We Fell Among Greeks, p. 123.

59. John Mulgan, Report on Experience (London: Oxford University Press, 1947), p.

CHAPTER II

1. L. I. Estin, Conditions in Greece (New York: The Irving Trust, 1946), pamphlet, p. 3.

2. Lanz, Partisan Warfare in the Balkans, pp. 11 - 12; German Anti-guerrilla Operations in the Balkans (1941-1944), DA Pamphlet No. 20-243 (Washington, 1954), p. 5.

3. Dr. Arthur Piske, Logistical Problems of the German Air Force in Greece: 1941-43 (Historical Division, Headquarters United States Army, Europe, 1953), p. 23.

4. Wehrmachtsbefehlshaber, Suedost (AOK 12) Abt 1a, Aktensammelheft, 164 Inf Div, 22.9.41 - 30.12.41 AOK 12. FRC Doc. No. 14749/15.

5. General der Flieger Wilhelm Speidel, Report on Greece (1942-44) (Historical Division, Headquarters United States Army, Europe, 1948) p. 65.

6. Unless otherwise specified, material in the following section has been taken primarily from Lanz, Partisan Warfare in the Balkans, pp. 44-53.

7. Testimony of Constantinos Triandaphylidis at the American Military Tribunal, 15 August 1947.

8. *Ibid*.

9. Woodhouse, *Apple of Discord*, pp. 44 - 45.

10. Hamson, *We Fell Among Greeks*, p. 149.

11. Woodhouse, *Apple of Discord*, p. 46.

12. C. M. Woodhouse, *European Resistance Movements, 1939-45* (New York, etc.: Pergamon Press, 1960), p. 381.

13. Hamson, *We Fell Among Greeks*, pp. 19 - 20.

14. Koutsoyiannopoulos was more precisely known as Prometheus II. Prometheus I having been Colonel Bakirdjis who had been forced to flee Athens because of Italian interest in his intelligence and resistance activities. Bakirdjis was subsequently associated with Colonel Psaros in EKKA and still later went over to EAM/ELAS.

15. Unless otherwise specified, material used for the balance of Chapter II has been taken mainly from the following sources: Myers, *Greek Entanglement*; Hamson, *We Fell Among Greeks*.

16. The sovereign was a coin containing 123.274 grains of gold, .9166 fine. Originally having a value of one pound sterling ($4.86), its value had increased with the inflated price of gold and its purchasing power in Greece was approximately $20. (Wines, A Lesson in Greek, p. 13.)

17. The strength figures quoted above are those given by E. C. W. Myers. Denys Hamson claims that Aris had about eighty men and Zervas approximately seventy.

18. Zervas' explanation of this self-promotion was that many officers junior to him had been promoted for their services with the Greek units serving under the British Middle East Command.

19. It was later learned that it had actually been seven weeks before a wooden tressle could be constructed and the viaduct put back in service. Meanwhile, all freight had to be unloaded north of the viaduct and trucked around to the southern side.

CHAPTER III

1. Unless otherwise specified, material in Chapter III has been taken primarily from the following sources: Myers, Greek Entanglement; Hamson, We Fell Among Greeks; Woodhouse, Apple of Discord.

2. Lanz, Partisan Warfare in the Balkans, pp. 65 - 66.

3. The four-pointed forms were not a new weapon, having been used in ancient times against foot troops and cavalry. The following definition is taken from Duane's Military Dictionary, published in 1810: "CALTROPS, in military affairs, is a piece of iron having four points, all disposed in a triangular form: so that 3 of them always rest upon the ground, and the 4th stands upwards in a perpendicular direction. Each point is 3 or 4 inches long. They are scattered over the ground and passages where the enemy is expected to march, especially the cavalry, in order to embarass their progress."

4. Lanz, Partisan Warfare in the Balkans, pp. 67 - 69.

5. Major Rufus Sheppard had been dropped in the Mount Olympus area to operate independently of Myers' mission, for reasons that have never been made clear. Sheppard fell completely under the spell of ELAS and continually sent glowing reports of that organization to SOE Cairo. He later came under the command of Myers but all efforts to convince him that ELAS was Communist dominated and playing a double game were unavailing. He died, a victim of an ELAS mine, still unconvinced.

6. Although Myers in Greek Entanglement uses the name Evmaios, Sarafis in his Greek Resistance Army always refers to Tzimas as Samariniotis. Apparently the EAM representative had more than one alias. In order to avoid confusion, this book will use Tzimas.

7. Sarafis, Greek Resistance Army, p. 43.

8. For the complete text of the first draft of the National Bands Agreement see Woodhouse, Apple of Discord, p. 298.

9. Sarafis, Greek Resistance Army, p. 60.

10. Unless otherwise specified, material in this section has been taken primarily from Sarafis, Greek Resistance Army.

11. Myers, Greek Entanglement, pp. 194 - 95.

12. Sarafis, Greek Resistance Army, p. 67.

13. The Germans also estimated the strength of EDES at 7,000 in July 1943 (DA Pamphlet 20-243, German Antiguerrilla Operations in the Balkans

(1941-1944), p. 38. In testimony before the American Military Tribunal at Nuernberg on 16 August 1947, p. 2092, Constantinos Triandaphylidis set EDES strength at 3,000 to 4,000 in March and 6,000 to 7,000 in July 1943.

14. Colonel Myers was promoted to Brigadier on or about 15 June.

15. Sarafis, Greek Resistance Army, p. 75.

16. McGlynn, Special Service in Greece, p. 29.

17. Trials of War Criminals before the Nuernberg Military Tribunals, vol. XI, case 7, U.S. vs List (Washington, 1950), p. 828.

18. For the complete text of the National Bands Agreement, see Woodhouse, Apple of Discord, pp. 299 - 300.

19. Myers, Greek Entanglement, p. 201.

20. Ibid., p. 221.

CHAPTER IV

1. A Luftwaffe field division was composed of air force personnel organized and operating as an infantry division.

2. DA Pamphlet 20-243, German Antiguerrilla Operations in the Balkans (1941-1944), pp. 41 - 42.

3. Description of the engagement at Leskovic is taken from Lanz, Partisan Warfare in the Balkans, pp. 56 - 58.

4. Sarafis, Greek Resistance Army, pp. 96 - 97.

5. McNeill, The Greek Dilemma, pp. 103 - 4.

6. Testimony of Constantinos Triandaphylidis at the American Military Tribunal, Nuerberg, 16 August 1947, p. 2092.

7. Woodhouse, Apple of Discord, p. 72.

8. Sarafis, Greek Resistance Army, p. 108.

9. Ibid., p. 112.

10. Ibid., p. 111.

11. Woodhouse, Apple of Discord, p. 167.

12. Sarafis, Greek Resistance Army, p. 119. This argument, being inconsistent with his statement of June 5th that EDES had only 500 men, casts further doubt on the accuracy of his previous figure.

13. Woodhouse was promoted to the rank of colonel in late 1943. According to Major Wines, the 26-year-old Woodhouse was the youngest colonel in the British Army.

14. Sarafis, Greek Resistance Army, p. 130.

15. Material in this section has been taken primarily from Lanz, Partisan Warfare in the Balkans.

16. Woodhouse, Apple of Discord, pp. 96 - 97; McNeill, The Greek Dilemma, p. 181.

17. Byford-Jones, The Greek Trilogy, p. 118; DA Pamphlet 20-243,

German Antiguerrilla Operations in the Balkans, p. 54; and Sarafis, Greek Resistance Army, p.

18. Woodhouse, Apple of Discord, p. 76.

19. Lanz, Partisan Warfare in the Balkans, pp. 17 - 18, 98 - 99.

20. Gen. Kdo. LXVIII A.K., Abt. 1a, Anlagen band Nr. 3 zum Ktb Nr. 3, 29 Sep - 20 Nov 1943, FRC 44058/4. Okdo H. Gr. E, Kriegstagebuch Nr. 4 1 July - 29 Sep 1944, FRC 65035/2.

21. Dr. Arthur J. W. Piske, Logistical Problems of the German Air Force in Greece: 1941-43, MS No. B-645 (Historical Division, Hq. United States Army, Europe, 1953), p. 50.

22. Woodhouse, Apple of Discord, pp. 77 - 80.

23. Wines, A Lesson in Greek, p. 37.

24. Ibid., pp. 48 - 49.

25. Sarafis, Greek Resistance Army, p. 148. Sarafis claims that EDES attacked ELAS on 25 January, precipitating the Epirus Team's counterattack.

26. Sarafis, Greek Resistance Army, p. 159.

27. Ibid., p. 164.

28. For the full text of the Plaka Armistice, see Woodhouse, Apple of Discord, pp. 303 - 4.

29. Material in this section has been taken primarily from Lanz, Partisan Warfare in the Balkans, pp. 94ff passim.

30. *Trials of War Criminals Before the Nuernberg Military Tribunals*, vol. XI, p. 971.

31. Ibid., p. 830.

32. Unless otherwise indicated material in the two following sections has been taken primarily from Gen. Kdo. LXVIII A.K., Kriegstagebuch Nr. 4, 1 Jan - 30 Jun 1944, FRC 549601 and DA Pamphlet 20-243, *German Anti-guerrilla Operations in the Balkans (1941-1944)*.

33. *Trials of War Criminals Before the Nuernberg Military Tribunals*, vol. XI, p. 1030.

34. The following descriptions of German reprisal actions are taken from *Trials of War Criminals Before the Nuernberg Military Tribunals*, vol. XI, pp. 831 - 33.

35. Mulgan, *Report on Experience*, p.

CHAPTER V

1. Woodhouse, *Apple of Discord*, p. 304.

2. Sarafis, *Greek Resistance Army*, pp. 169 - 70.

3. Wines, A Lesson in Greek, pp. 169 - 70.

4. Sarafis, *Greek Resistance Army*, p. 172.

5. Wines, A Lesson in Greek, p. 200.

6. Seton-Watson, The East European Revolution, pp. 137 - 38.

7. McNeill, The Greek Dilemma, p. 97.

8. Sarafis, Greek Resistance Army, p. 70.

9. Wines, A Lesson in Greek, p. 163.

10. D. O. W. Hall, Escapes (Wellington, N.Z.: Pamphlet published by the War History Branch, Department of Internal Affairs, 1954), p. 14.

11. John Mulgan, Report on Experience, pp. 100 - 1.

12. Woodhouse, Apple of Discord, p. 99n.

13. Sir Reginald Leeper, When Greek Meets Greek (London: Chatto and Windus, 1950), p. 23.

14. McNeill, The Greek Dilemma, p. 128.

15. Sarafis, Greek Resistance Army, p. 178.

16. For the complete text of the Lebanon Charter see Woodhouse, Apple of Discord, p. 305.

17. Woodhouse, Apple of Discord, p. 192.

18. DA Pamphlet 20-243, German Antiguerrilla Operations in the Balkans, pp. 59 - 60.

19. Material on Operation STEINADLER has been taken primarily from Lanz, Partisan Warfare in the Balkans, pp. 107ff; Army Group E, War Diary, 1 Jul - 29 Sep 1944, FRC 65035/2; DA Pamphlet 20-243, German Antiguerrilla

Operations in the Balkans, pp. 70 - 72.

20. The figure of 6,000 to 8,000 guerrillas with the 9th Division is slightly higher than the ELAS claim of 5,500 and is much higher than the total estimated by the ALO's in that area. According to Major Wines there were only 1,200 to 1,500 active ELAS andartes with the 9th Division. (Wines, A Lesson in Greek, p. 165.)

21. McNeill, The Greek Dilemma, p. 145.

22. Woodhouse, Apple of Discord, p. 112.

23. Sarafis, Greek Resistance Army, p. 223.

24. Woodhouse, Apple of Discord, p. 199.

25. Material on Operation KREUZOTTER has been obtained from Army Group E, War Diary, 1 July - 29 September 1944, FRC No. 65035/2. Material contained in DA Pamphlet 20-243, German Antiguerrilla Operations in the Balkans, is largely incorrect, having been based on projected German plans rather than actual operations.

26. Sarafis, Greek Resistance Army, pp. 235 - 36.

27. Ibid., p. 235.

CHAPTER VI

1. DA Pamphlet 20-243, German Antiguerrilla Operations in the Balkans, p. 62.

2. Sarafis, Greek Resistance Army, p. 170. For a description of the organization and activities of ELAN, see Ibid., pp. 280 - 85.

3. Byford-Jones, The Greek Trilogy, p. 93.

4. DA Pamphlet 20-243, German Antiguerrilla Operations in the Balkans, p. 63.

5. Lanz, Partisan Warfare in the Balkans, pp. 19 - 20.

6. Woodhouse, Apple of Discord, p. 208.

7. Wines, A Lesson in Greek, pp. 228 - 29.

8. Woodhouse, Apple of Discord, p. 204.

9. Byford-Jones, The Greek Trilogy, p. 97.

10. For the complete text of the Caserta Agreement, see Woodhouse, Apple of Discord, pp. 306 - 7.

11. Ehrman, Grand Strategy, Vol. VI, p. 61.

12. Mary E. Williams, Compiler, Chronology 1941-1945, U.S. Army in World War II, Special Studies (Washington, 1960), p. 262.

13. Unless otherwise specified, material in the following section has been taken primarily from Williams, Chronology, pp. 275ff.

14. Ehrman, Grand Strategy, Vol. VI, p. 44.

15. McNeill, The Greek Dilemma, p. 150; Woodhouse, Apple of Discord, p. 204.

16. Wines, A Lesson in Greek, pp. 228 - 29.

17. Geoffrey Chandler, The Divided Land (London: Macmilan & Co., Ltd., 1959), pp. 24 - 25.

18. "But the guerrillas, aided by the Allied Balkans Air Forces, killed perhaps some 5,000 men, wounded and captured as many more, and destroyed or captured perhaps a hundred locomotives and five hundred vehicles, together with arms and ammuntion." Ehrman, Grand Strategy, Vol. VI, p. 45.

19. Personelle Blutige Verluste, Der Heeresarrt im Oberkommando des Heeres, Gen. St. d. H./ Gen. Qu. im Verluste der Wehrmacht bis 1944 (H 1/176).

20. Woodhouse, Apple of Discord, p. 203.

21. Ibid., pp. 90 - 91, 208.

22. Ibid., p. 211.

23. Seton-Watson, The East European Revolution, p. 318.

24. "X" was a violently anticommunist political organization formed in Athens during the last months of the German occupation. Led by Colonel Grivas, the military arm of X never engaged in combatting the Germans but directed its entire energies to opposing EAM/ELAS.

25. McNeill, The Greek Dilemma, pp. 156 - 57.

26. Sarafis, Greek Resistance Army, pp. 291 - 92.

27. Leeper, When Greek Meets Greek, p. 93.

28. Ehrman, Grand Strategy, Vol. VI, p. 61.

29. Unless otherwise specified material in this section has been taken primarily from McNeill, The Greek Dilemma, pp. 154 - 65; Sarafis, Greek Resistance Army, pp. 293 - 304.

30. Winston S. Churchill, The Second World War, Triumph and Tragedy (Cambridge, Mass.: The Riverside Press, 1953), pp. 287 - 88.

31. George Siantos as secretary of KKE was the real head of the Communist Party of Greece. He had replaced Tzimas as political advisor to GHQ, ELAS and had later become Secretary of Home Affairs under PEEA.

32. McNeill, The Greek Dilemma, p. 165.

33. Material in the following section has been taken primarily from Leeper, When Greek Meets Greek, pp. 100 - 15; McNeill, The Greek Dilemma, pp. 165 - 79; and Woodhouse, Apple of Discord, pp. 217 - 18.

34. The figure of seven killed is taken from McNeill, The Greek Dilemma, but others -- including EAM - claimed from 10 to 22 killed and 60 to 100 wounded. Opposing views on the provocation of the firing are also presented. See: Byford-Jones, The Greek Trilogy, pp. 138-44; Richard Capell, Simiomata, A Greek Note Book, pp. 121 - 22, 135 - 36; and the New York Times, December 4 and 6, 1944.

35. Material in the following section has been taken primarily from: Leeper, When Greek Meets Greek, pp. 115 - 18; McNeill, The Greek Dilemma, pp. 179 - 85; and Woodhouse, Apple of Discord, pp. 222-23.

36. Unless otherwise specified, material in the following section has been taken primarily from Sarafis, Greek Resistance Army, pp. 304 - 13.

37. Lanz, Partisan Warfare in the Balkans, pp. 19 - 20.

38. Woodhouse, Apple of Discord, p. 82.

39. Byford-Jones, The Greek Trilogy, p. 197.

40. Material in the following section has been taken primarily from Churchill, Triumph and Tragedy, pp. 313 - 24.

41. McNeill, The Greek Dilemma, p. 188.

42. Unless otherwise specified, material in the following section has been taken primarily from NcNeill, The Greek Dilemma, pp. 165, 188 - 90.

43. Leeper, When Greek Meets Greek, p. 118.

44. Woodhouse, Apple of Discord, p. 218.

45. Capell, Simiomata, p. 190n.

46. Unless otherwise specified, material in the following section has been taken primarily from McNeill, The Greek Dilemma, pp. 194 - 97 and Woodhouse, Apple of Discord, pp. 226 - 30.

47. For the complete text of the Varkiza Agreement, see: Woodhouse, Apple of Discord, pp. 308 - 10.

www.ingramcontent.com/pod-product-compliance
Lightning Source LLC
Chambersburg PA
CBHW081832170426
43199CB00017B/2706